To Me I Thee Wed

Be Your Own Better Half

Discover How to Love, Honor and Cherish Yourself Forever After

Julia Bowlin, M.D.

JoBri
Press

JoBri Press, Ltd
www.JobriPress.com

TO ME I THEE WED © 2013 by Julia Bowlin, M.D

Books may be purchased in quantity by contacting the publisher directly: JoBri Press 937-548-6830

Printed in the United States of America

First Printing: 2013

Editing and Interior Dan Teck. Cover Design Lloyd Lelina
Bowlin M.D., Julia A
          To ME I Thee Wed: Be Your Own Better Half
ISBN: 978-0-9883053-0-4(Paperback) LCCN Pending
ISBN: 978-0-9883053-1-1 (e-book)

          1.   Self-Help   2. Health and Fitness

This book is dedicated to my husband, Rick.

*Thank you, Rick, for having faith in me—and in us—
even when my own faith faltered.*

*Thank you for being my friend
and for helping me be my own best friend.*

*Thank you for loving me,
even when I questioned my own worth.*

Contents

Preface

An Enlightened Blunder

~ The Best Ideas Come When You Least Expect Them ~

Some people say there are no mistakes. So I'll call it a stroke of unintended insight that overtook my nephew during his wedding vows. He and his bride dutifully recited their lines exactly as the priest said them—with one exception: When it came time for Matthew to say, "I marry thee," what came out instead was, "I marry *me*."

If he could go back in time, I'm sure he would have said it correctly—but I'm glad he didn't! I loved *his* version! Aside from providing a moment of levity (and mild embarrassment), I thought it was the perfect message—for me, for him, and perhaps for the entire world.

The more I reflected on this little slip, the more I realized how inspiring it was. It got me thinking: *What if we could* all *make loving vows—not just to our spouses, but also to* ourselves? *What if we all committed to giving* ourselves *the lifelong,*

> ## What if...
> *we all committed to giving ourselves the lifelong, unconditional love that we seek from others? What if we could be our own ideal partners?*

unconditional love that we seek from others? What if we could be our own ideal partners?

While none of these questions in any way diminished the joy of the occasion, I couldn't shake the thought that my nephew had inadvertently stumbled upon something very profound.

For weeks after Matthew's wedding, his phrase kept circling around my head. And the more I thought about it, the more I saw love and relationships in a different light.

I saw couples trying to fit their partners into fantasy-molds rather than appreciating the reality of who they actually were. I saw single people feeling like their only chance at happiness depended on finding a mate. And I saw people of all kinds looking for others to provide what was missing inside them (or, more accurately, what *wasn't* missing—what they only *thought* was missing!).

In all of these instances, the outcome was the same: disappointment.

What makes these scenarios especially heartbreaking is that all of these people—like all of us—already have access to a lifetime supply of love. And this love doesn't depend on a spouse, a parent, or anyone else.

A World of "To Me I Thee Wed"

After Matthew's wedding, I spent a lot of time contemplating how many people lacked self-love; but I also had an encouraging inner knowing: I knew that everyone had the potential to experience this deep love, and that this experience could transform not only individuals but the entire world.

I imagined a world raised on the concept of self-love, a world in which practicing self-care was as accepted as seeking a mate (or even just a date). I know this idea may seem corny to some people, but see if you can share a vision of this world:

Imagine people at the hair salon, "gossiping" about how they had tapped into a new level of self-understanding. Imagine movie theaters showing the latest "romances," in which the stars find inner love, which then bubbles over to everyone around them. Imagine parents beseeching their adult children—asking not, "When are you going to give me a grandchild?" but rather, "When are you going to listen to the dictates of your own heart?"

I wish we already lived in this world where all parents instilled self-love within us, where all teachers and coaches taught us to uncover our individual talents and passions, and where we all encouraged one another to reach our goals of self-fulfillment. For now this is just a vision, but I truly hope and believe that we can move toward this ideal.

Until that ideal world arrives, however, I've decided to play the role of those supportive hairdressers, uplifting movies, and encouraging parents. I'll apply gentle, loving pressure to all those who need encouragement to seek love within themselves. And I'm starting right here and now, in this book! I'll be your cheerleader, your confidante, your accountability partner, your guide, your friend and your fellow traveler on this journey to your fullest, most loving life—and the fullest, most loving YOU!

My Unconventional Conventional Story

Since we're going to be taking this journey together, I'll share a little bit about my own journey toward self-love.

From the outside my life might look fairly conventional: I've been married for over 21 years, my husband and I have two children, and I put my pants on the same way you do. I have a private family medical practice in Ohio. I work hard, go to church on "Somedays" and to my kids' sports games on other days, and still find time to clip my toenails in between somehow.

From the inside, however, life has not always been so smooth. I know what it is like to feel completely divorced from myself and my purpose. From a young age, I experienced various forms of mishandling, emotional neglect and denial, sexual abuse, and self-inflicted trauma. As a young adult, I had to work hard to overcome an eating disorder and other unhealthy behaviors. And my marriage, as loving and nurturing as it is, has certainly had its share of ups and downs—including a two-year separation.

All of these experiences, however painful and challenging, have helped forge my character and taught me about my capacity for forgiveness, personal growth, and self-love. I've had to learn how to be strong and independent yet also vulnerable and open to receiving help, care, and love. I've had to balance work, family, and marriage without losing myself (something that has not always come naturally to me). And I've had to admit that I, too, am a fallible, imperfect human—doing my best to learn, grow, and share as best as I can in my family and in my professional life.

This has not always been an easy journey. I've taken plenty of missteps and wrong turns, and I'm still a work in progress—like all of us. But I hope that by sharing what I have learned and experienced, I can help to open your heart to the possibilities for joy, fulfillment, and unconditional love.

Different People with the Same Needs

I understand that everyone's experience with love is different. Some people may have had a consistent source of love showered upon them throughout their life, while others never received any at all. But even if you've never known true love before, even if you didn't get enough love (or a *healthy* enough love) as a child, you still have just as much potential to experience love as anyone else.

Regardless of our past (or present), almost all of us have to learn to give ourselves the self-love and self-care we so dearly need—yet all too often neglect. Time and again I've seen friends, family members, and patients give so much of their time and energy to others—to their families, churches, students, and all the other people in their lives—yet when it comes to their own health and well-being, they struggle to follow through with even the most basic self-care. I have known very intelligent professors, successful businessmen and women, and yes, even physicians who struggle with issues of self-neglect and self-harm.

No matter your education level, financial status, marital status, or sexual preference, we are all human beings with core needs. Although these needs are basic, they often elude us during the insanity we call daily life. Needs such as a nurturing understanding of who we are and what we need from ourselves and from others. Needs such as a loving touch, eye contact, or a warm smile. Needs such as a supportive word when we feel the most vulnerable. And the need for self-love and self-care. Until we can identify these needs and acknowledge how they are being met (or not), we won't feel fulfilled intellectually, physically, and emotionally—or be the best person we can.

Who is This Book For?

This book is for everyone who has neglected to give themselves the love and care they deserve. It is not only for people who are single or haven't experienced love. It is for anyone who would like to feel even *more* love—starting from within. It is for everyone who has ever felt burned out from over-giving without taking time to refill their own cup. It is for everyone who has ever wanted to be whole, fulfilled, and unconditionally loved. It is for anyone who could benefit from learning to love, honor, and cherish themselves.

This book is for you.

I mean this from the depth of my heart.

My Wish for You

My wish for you is that, while reading this book, all of you—especially those who have struggled the most to find love of all kinds—will be able to uncover a deep, true, all-encompassing source of self-love in all its wonderment.

Please take the time to read this book with an open heart and an attitude of grace. There will be places in this book that are repetitive and some parts that may not be relevant for you at this moment, but I assure you there will be other places that will give you some serious *a-ha* moments. If you can come away with even a single life-changing moment, then the book will be worth your time.

Thank you for sharing this journey with me—and, most importantly, with yourself.

Many blessings,

Julia Bowlin, M.D.

March 2013

Introduction

Something Old, Something New

~ Being Your Own Ideal Partner ~

I always knew who my perfect partner would be: handsome, sleek, macho, strong and athletic—someone who would live to serve me endlessly and do everything I wanted to do every day...and, of course, never pass gas in the bed!

What's YOUR vision of an ideal partner?

Someone who loves you unconditionally? Someone who always supports you and has your back? Someone who sees you, understands you, "gets" you? Someone who can be tender and calm or wild and forthright when you need them to be? Someone you can really be yourself with?

Maybe you imagine your ideal partner as someone who shares your values, your interests, and your tastes. Or you might see this person as someone who is completely devoted to you, totally committed—someone who will be there for you through thick and thin, richer or poorer, in sickness and in health, for the rest of your life.

This person could be your spouse and/or a best friend, but they could also be someone even closer to you—the person with whom you have the most intimate, long-lasting relationship of your entire life: *YOU!*

What if *you* could give yourself everything that you would hope for in an ideal husband, wife, or partner? What if *you're* the person who could always support you, value you, make you laugh, and love you unconditionally? What if you could cheer yourself on during your victories *and* your defeats, forgive yourself when you slip up, and be your own best friend *all* the time?

What if you could be your own ideal partner?

Would this mean that you couldn't be married or in a relationship?

Not at all! In fact, it's just the opposite: Giving yourself the love and support you deserve makes it *easier* to be in a relationship. You don't have to be needy—because you fulfill your own needs. You don't blame your partner—because you take personal responsibility for your own life. You don't expect someone else to complete you—because you're already complete. And you have more to give to others—because you fill your own cup...until it overflows!

Let me state unequivocally that this book is NOT anti-marriage! I have been married for over 21 years. My husband and I have grown together (and sometimes apart), we are raising two wonderful (and sometimes wonderfully challenging) children, and we've shared many of life's ups and downs (and occasional crashes) with love, compromise, and support. After all this time, we're moving into more love than ever, we're completely devoted to one another, and we're looking forward to spending the rest of our lives together.

Don't get me wrong—sometimes marriage or commitment to another person can be like a bulldozer heading your way. You have a choice: stay and work through the rough stuff or move (leave the relationship) before you are scooped up with all the other shit that life throws in the scooper with you! But based on my experience, I believe that marriage or any other life-long romantic commitment, although not essential for happiness, can be among the greatest blessings of life—and can offer some of life's greatest lessons.

If you are married or in a serious relationship (even if it's with your dog), the *To Me I Thee Wed* (TMITW) approach is perfect for you. More than likely, your partner will thank you for giving yourself love and support. Self-assured individuals are not threatened by other people's empowerment. If they truly want the best for you, they will be glad to see you grow as a person, gain more self-confidence, reach your potential, and be passionate about your growing sense of purpose and sense of self!

This perspective shift is also helpful if you are divorced, widowed, or aren't currently in a relationship.

If you have lost a spouse or significant other to death or divorce, you know the pain of separation. You know the difficulty of shifting your perspective from "we" to "me." You know that the journey of emotional healing is a process.

As someone who has been through a marital separation (as well as years of being single) I know the importance of standing on your own two feet, providing for your own inner and outer needs, and being a whole person. If you have been on your own, you know how important it is to be strong. You have had to face the world—and yourself—on your own. You have met challenges, recovered from setbacks, and survived!

But now it's time to do more than just survive—it's your time to thrive!

It's your time to feel fulfilled. It's your time to love yourself. It's your time to be your own best friend, your own cheerleader and champion, your own ideal partner.

But how do you start?

It's easy to find places to look for a date or a mate (e.g., online dating sites, singles bars, and social events), but where do you turn when you're looking to commit to a relationship with *yourself?* What's the personal-growth equivalent of a matchmaker or a singles bar? Where are the models for this journey of self-love and personal empowerment?

Following the path of self-love might not come naturally to you. After all, it is a significant shift from what we've been taught. Most of us have received the message passed along for generations: *You need someone else to complete you.*

It's been ingrained into our expectations that every little girl should dream of marrying her Prince Charming. Or you may have been given the message that a "trophy wife" is a measure of a man's worth. You might have been told that, if you are married, your husband will provide for you, or your wife will take care of you. Your spouse will fill the void within you and, likewise, *you* are responsible for *their* self-esteem.

You've probably also been programmed with negative stereotypes of marriage: "the ball and chain"—as well as gender stereotypes, such as the nagging wife and the emotionally unavailable husband.

How do we reverse centuries of cultural programming?

Fortunately, the path to self-love has been carved out by the traditional path to marriage! By applying the steps of an external romantic relationship to your own individual life, you can discover how to feel loved, honored, and cherished—whether or not you're married!

The To Me I Thee Wed *"Marriage" Process*

In this book, we'll take "something old" (the traditional path of marriage) and apply it to something relatively new: the concept of self-love and self-care. This may seem like plain old common sense (and perhaps even a bit corny); however, it's one thing to understand the need for self-love and self-care, and quite another to practice it.

Throughout the chapters of this book, you'll follow the steps of a developing romantic relationship, applying each step to your own personal growth and self-love:

- **Meeting, Flirting, and Dating** – You'll find the spark within yourself, build your interest in your own life, and get to know yourself more intimately and lovingly than ever before.

- **Love and Engagement** – You'll allow your acceptance of inner love to grow as you become increasingly and purposefully engaged in your own life.

- **Wedding Planning and Preparation** – Thinking about all parts of a traditional wedding will help you clarify *your* style, tastes, values...in short, who YOU really are.

- **The Big Day** – At the heart of your "TMITW" journey, you will create, express, and internalize your vow to love, honor, and cherish yourself as long as you live.

- **The Wedding Night and the Honeymoon** – You'll celebrate your love and commitment to yourself—with a personal get-away, which can be as far away as a tropical island or as close as an afternoon at the local spa. Wherever you go, you will find a place of personal safety where you can honor your needs and uncover your true self.

- **Married Life** – Although there's so much focus on the wedding itself (in this book and in our culture), it's only a single day—while a marriage or other other committed relationships are intended to last the rest of your life! By exploring the elements of a successful marriage (including the challenges that tend to arise), you'll discover how to make your own "marriage" with your true self a joyful, fulfilling, and loving one forever after— as long as you shall live!

- **Separation and Return** – Whether or not you literally get separated or divorced, almost every relationship has periods when you're not as close as you'd like to be—and that includes your relationship with yourself. Find out what to do when you lose that connection with your true self—and renew your commitment to love yourself.

At every step of the way, you'll discover how to give yourself the same level of love and commitment that you would give to (and hope to receive from) your ideal partner.

Giving yourself the love you deserve might come very naturally to you. On the other hand, you might feel nervous or uncomfortable with the concept of focusing on your own wants, needs, and desires. Practicing self-care might feel odd or foreign—perhaps even *wrong* in some way. At some point in the process, you may even find yourself wondering:

Isn't this selfish?

The short answer is: NO!

What IS selfish, however, is NOT giving yourself unconditional love! It's selfish *not* to give yourself self-care, not to give yourself ME-time, and not to give yourself what you want, need, and deserve!

Although it's often praised as "selfless," self-denial is extremely selfish—because it implies that you expect others to give you what you want. You expect others to provide for you. You expect others to "complete" you.

And if they don't, you resent them. You'll be in a bad mood or run-down and empty. If you don't fill yourself up, you'll have nothing to give others—and you won't be much fun to be around!

If you define "selfish" as "not giving," then *not* giving to yourself is the height of this negative kind of selfishness. On the other hand, if the opposite of this negative selfishness is "giving," then the ideal would be giving so much to yourself that you can give to others from your overflow—as you overflow with an abundance of joy, energy, and other gifts that you share freely and naturally.

That said...

Looking at it another way, however, *yes*, self-love IS selfish! It is "sagaciously selfish"!

Sagacious Selfishness

The wisest sages know that self-actualization is not about self-denial—it's about becoming and expressing your fullest, most glorious self. And that's what "sagacious selfishness" means. It's a *healthy* selfishness, a way of thinking and acting that shows a deep appreciation and concern for yourself.

Being sagaciously selfish means that you respect your own feelings, desires, and needs, and that you trust your knowledge, ability, and experience. It means nurturing yourself and loving yourself unconditionally. It means asking for emotional support without apology. On a physical level, it means doing such things as eating when you're hungry, resting when you're tired, or using the bathroom when you need to!

People who practice sagacious selfishness have a zest, a verve for living, a natural joy that comes from honoring their inherent value.

Sagacious Selfishness

Sagacious
wise; sage-like; displaying acute mental discernment

Selfishness
devotion to caring for oneself; concern with one's own interests and welfare

Sagacious Selfishness
feeling self-love and practicing self-care; respecting your feelings, desires, and needs; nurturing yourself and loving yourself unconditionally

Healthy selfishness opens the door to a life of freedom—freedom from being ruled by the opinions and demands of others, as well as freedom from the voices in your own mind (often left over from childhood) that judge and blame you unfairly.

Self-Denial

The opposite of sagacious selfishness is unhealthy self-denial, which often stems from having your childhood needs unmet or disregarded. Feeling ignored or unappreciated, you may have formed the false belief that your wants and needs aren't as important as others'—that *you* don't really matter. You might end up feeling guilty just for having basic human wants, needs, and desires.

If carried into adulthood, such beliefs lead to anxiety, indecisiveness, rage, or depression. They can also lead to unfair or unrealistic expectations—especially if you harbor fantasies about a romantic "savior" swooping in to fill the void, finally giving you the love and care you were unfairly denied as a child. And while such fantasies can make for wonderful movies, they tend to interfere with a healthy experience of reality.

Fantasy vs. Reality

As you read on, you'll see that one of the recurring themes of the TMITW journey is *Fantasy vs. Reality*.

We've all been force-fed cultural fantasies about love, romance, and marriage. And we all have our own individual fantasies. Many of these can be very positive—hopes, dreams, and visions that lead you toward goals and self-fulfillment. Other fantasies, however, may be unrealistic—leading to disappointment or robbing you of the enjoyment of what *actually is* when it doesn't match your fantasy of what you thought "should" be.

As you take this journey, you'll trade expectations for experience. And, hopefully, you'll find that reality can be more rewarding and enriching than even the grandest fantasy.

The Lollipop Principle

As a final note before we begin this journey, I'd like to look at two approaches that you can take to this book: You can read it straight through (like a novel), or you can also do the exercises at the end of each chapter.

There's nothing wrong with either approach. I truly hope that you do enjoy reading the book. I want it to be a page-turner! Hopefully you'll find it entertaining, enjoyable, and perhaps even enlightening.

But if you don't apply any of it to your life—if you merely enjoy the book while you're reading it, then close it and go back to living exactly the same way—then the book will be like a lollipop for you: something that you enjoy while you're having it, but that provides no lasting value once it's done.

And that's OK. Lollipops are fun. They taste good. And we all need things in our lives that are purely for in-the-moment enjoyment.

My hope for this book, however, is that it's more than just a "lollipop" for you. I hope that it is like a delicious, healthy meal— one that you enjoy while you're eating it but that also provides nourishment, makes you stronger and healthier, and perhaps even opens your eyes (and palate) to a whole new lifestyle—one that embraces the mindset that things can be enjoyable *and* healthful, as opposed to the either/or mindset (e.g., it either tastes great but it's bad for me, or it's healthy but disgusting).

In short, I hope that you will be an active participant, fully engaged (yes, pun intended) in your own journey of self-love at every step of the way.

I want you to experience first-hand just how invigorating, empowering, and FUN it is to practice self-care. I want you to experience first-hand how much your life transforms when you give yourself the same degree of commitment and unconditional love that you would want from an ideal partner. And I want you to experience this love not just during the few hours or days that you're reading this book but for the rest of your life.

After all, you deserve it.

Chapter One

Meeting and Flirting

~ Lighting the Spark of Self-Love ~

I had just finished my first week of med school, and I was already feeling overwhelmed. On top of the workload, everything and everyone was new to me—no familiar faces, no emotional support network, not even a study buddy! So I was thrilled when I made my first friend, and even more thrilled when she invited me to go bowling with a group of guys she'd just met.

As I walked into the bowling alley, I could feel the whole place buzzing with the hustle-bustle of crashing pins and social electricity. I've never been the world's most socially confident person, and the crowded, noisy scene made me literally shake with nervous anxiety. Despite my earlier enthusiasm, the prospect of meeting a group of boisterous strangers suddenly seemed unnerving, and I wondered if I should just turn around and retreat to the safety of the library.

As soon as I met my new bowling buddies, however, all of my stress seemed to evaporate. They were warm and welcoming, and instantly made me feel like one of the gang. One of the first people I met was a tall gentleman with graying hair, a gentle disposition, and an infectious joy. When he introduced himself as Ricky Bowlin, I assumed he was joking (since they were all *bowlin'*); so my first words to him were, "Yeah, right!" But he promptly pointed up to the screen where all of the bowlers' names were displayed. Sure enough, right there in front of me was the name *Ricky Bowlin*.

Ricky was having a difficult time hitting the pins that night—possibly due to the excitement of meeting me (although it may have been because he'd had a few drinks). Whatever the cause, I quickly diagnosed his classic case of "gutter-itis" and prescribed a cure: I told him that if he jumped up three times, rubbed his belly, patted his head twice, and spun around 10 times that he would be sure to hit the pins. Like an obedient patient, Ricky dutifully followed my prescription to a T. Sure enough, his next roll was a strike!

Thus began a romance that, within just a few short years, would turn *me* into a Bowlin!

The Spark

I have such fond memories of that night. Aside from the excitement of my first social outing since starting med school and the funny coincidence about the "Bowlin" alley, I was so taken by the fact that a man who didn't even know me was willing to take my frivolous suggestion—and act it out with such good-natured enthusiasm. It's amazing to think that decades of profound love, marriage, and children were set in motion by a moment of such silly, lighthearted fun!

It may not have been the classic "love at first sight"—an instant inferno of passion—but it was the spark that eventually burst into flames and grew into a warm fire of lasting love.

Spark for Yourself!

This "Spark Principle" doesn't just hold true for romantic potential with others. It applies to many areas of life: creative projects (the moment when you get an idea), business ventures (the moment when you recognize that a business opportunity has potential), and even books (the moment when a book grabs you—maybe while you're hearing about it, reading the back cover, or flipping through at random—and you decide, "I'm going to read this. I may not love it or even make it all the way through, but I'll at least give it a try.").

More importantly than any of these sparks, however, is the spark you feel for your own life.

Have you ever felt a spark of potential within yourself? Have you ever had a moment when you thought, "Yes, I can do this," or even, "I don't know if I can do this, but I'm going to give it a try"? Have you had a moment when you took an interest in your own life—when you recognized the potential to stretch beyond what you've done and who you've been? A moment when you decided, "I'm interesting" or "I'm worth it"?

That's how self-love starts: by recognizing or *feeling* the potential within yourself. It doesn't mean you're conceited—it means you acknowledge your own inherent worth. You get a sense that you're someone worth spending time with, someone special, someone with a spark.

> **Have you ever felt a spark of potential within yourself? Have you ever had a moment when you thought, "Yes, I can do this," or even, "I don't know if I can do this, but I'm going to give it a try"?**

Being Open to Self-Love

We all know that romantic love can strike you at any time. Love can find you in an office building, in a shopping mall, on a mountaintop, in a bowling alley, or anywhere else you may find yourself—and often where you least expect it. And beware: Cupid can be sneaky! He's known to shoot his arrows into your back, so you don't even see it coming—and by the time it strikes, there's nothing you can do to stop it!

Also, love often shows up in unexpected forms—often very different from our preconceived notions of what it "should" be. It might look nothing like the images you've had in your head. It might feel nothing like you ever imagined it would. It might bear no resemblance to the romantic movies you've seen or books you've read or fantasies you've conjured up in your own mind. (How many people have passed up a chance at love simply because it didn't show up on a white horse carrying roses and chocolate?)

Likewise, the inner spark of potential self-love can ignite at any time—and in many different ways and forms. It might be triggered by a chance encounter, a conversation with a friend, a song on the radio, or by a book (perhaps even this one!). It can be a dramatic moment when you finally say "Enough!"—and stop putting up with mistreatment (by others or by yourself). Or it can emerge slowly and quietly from a deep inner yearning for something more.

Response-ability

The truth response-ability is that you don't always have a choice about if, when, or how a spark will show up—with yourself, with others, in romance, or in any other area of your life. Sometimes you feel it, sometimes you don't. That's part of the magic and mystery of love and life.

But you always have the ability to choose your response to sparks (or anything else, for that matter). Do you fan the fire, or blow it out? Do you pour water or oil on it? Or do you just walk away and ignore it altogether?

It's your choice. It's always your choice.

And if you don't feel a spark (within yourself or in any area of your life), you can choose to stick around—to see if one starts, or to try to start one yourself. Just the fact that you're willing to see if a spark shows up is bit of a spark in itself—a sign that you recognize some potential!

RESPONSE-ABILITY
The ability to choose your response
(to ANY situation)

So, do you already feel a spark within yourself? Can you recognize the potential for something more, the desire for something more—for more fulfillment, joy, and love? Are you willing to explore, to give yourself a shot?

If you're ready to take this ride, great! If you're not 100% on board, don't worry—you don't have to be! I'm not asking you to start "picking out the china" or to make a lifelong commitment right away. I'm just asking you to be open to exploring the potential within yourself—to flirt with the possibility that there's something more. Just like you would do if you met someone and felt a spark—you'd flirt.

Flirting

Whether you're single or in a relationship, you've certainly flirted—and been flirted with—at some point in your life. Oftentimes, flirting is nothing more than a casual, playful interaction; but it's also how people seek out potential mates.

Flirting isn't just for romantic situations, though. You can flirt with greatness...or with disaster. You can flirt with an idea. You can even flirt with yourself and your own potential! Flirting is simply hinting at the possibility of greater intimacy—the potential for something more.

Body Language and Nonverbal Communication

Researchers estimate that 93% of all communication is nonverbal: 38% vocal quality (volume, pitch, tone, and rhythm) and 55% body language (movements, posture, and facial expressions), with only 7% of communication being based on the words themselves.[1] Perhaps nowhere is this more evident than with flirtation.

When you're flirting, it's not so much *what* you say that matters, but *how* you say it. For instance, "It's nice to meet you," can be coldly professional, polite yet distant, or charming and seductive—depending on your tone of voice, the type of smile that does (or doesn't) accompany the words, physical proximity, and a host of other nonverbal cues, such as the following:

> *Communication is 93% Nonverbal!*
> - *55% body language*
> - *38% vocal quality*
> - *7% the actual words*

---

[1] Borg, James. *Body Language: 7 Easy Lessons to Master the Silent Language*. FT Press, 2010

- **Eye Contact** – for more than a second and/or repeatedly making eye contact (without staring—which can be unnerving or downright creepy!)

- **Entering "Personal Space"** – While the exact amount may vary from culture to culture (and person to person), you can generally tell when someone is *literally* keeping their distance—or, on the opposite side of the spectrum, "invading" your personal space in an undesired way.

- **Initiating Conversation** – not necessarily a "pick-up" line—just any opening that invites someone to talk.

- **"Open" Body Language** – Physical cues such as keeping one's feet pointed at the other person, mirroring gestures and movements, and NOT crossing your arms can send the message that someone is interested.

- **Casual Touching** – such as "accidentally" brushing up against someone or briefly touching their forearm during a conversation (NOT groping or inappropriate touching!). A person's reaction to such a touch (withdrawing, or responding with a similar touch) can be a fairly clear indicator of their level of interest and the possibility of greater intimacy.

- **Animated Movement** – Flirters tend to be more animated with their gestures while talking, incorporating much more hand and body movement into their conversations.

- **Animated Vocal Tone** – As with movement, a more lively vocal tone (inflections, changes in pitch and volume, etc.) can indicate that someone is interested and engaged. (By contrast, consider someone speaking in a low-volume monotone—probably not looking to "take it to the next level"!)

- **Compliments/Flattery** – By giving someone a forthright compliment, you indicate your interest without actually hitting on them or "making a move." As with all other types of flirtation, however, the *way* the compliment is delivered generally indicates more than the compliment itself. (Maybe they're interested in fashion and just really love your outfit—no flirtation intended.)

Despite these and many other signs of possible flirtation, flirting is not generally something that we need to analyze. You don't have to check the angle of someone's feet or measure their distance from you to know if there's potential interest. You don't have to watch for briefly raised eyebrows or keep track of how often they touch their hair to gauge someone's level of attraction. Most people (who aren't completely inept at picking up social cues) can tell whether or not someone is flirting.

You just know.

And you know when you are flirting with someone. When you flirt, you're genuinely interested in someone. You feel a spark—something that you might want to explore. And you want to put your best self forward. Not a "phony" self, but your most alluring self. You with the volume turned up on your most charming aspects—and turned down on any parts you're not particularly proud of (or simply anything that you don't want to "lead" with). You at your most attractive.

So, how does all of this apply to you as an individual?

Even if you're happily married, in a committed relationship, or happily single, you can benefit from learning the art of flirting. No, I'm not advising that married/committed people go out and flirt with strangers—or anyone (other than their partners), for that matter! What I am suggesting is that there are aspects of flirting that can bring you to life, make you more vibrant and animated, make you more fully engaged (with others and with yourself), and make you feel more alive—more fully YOU!

Many parts of flirting—such as compliments/flattery, animated movement and vocal tone, and a positive interest—can be applied to yourself as an individual. For instance, ask yourself:

- **How do you talk to yourself?** Does your inner voice build you up with compliments, flattery, and encouraging affirmations—or do you tear yourself down with criticism? Do you speak to yourself as you would to a child or an adult? In a respectful or critical manner? Do you encourage your attempt to better yourself, or shoot down your own dreams and aspirations?

- **How do you view yourself?** Are you critical of your appearance, behavior, and other traits and qualities, or do you feel good about who you are? Do you have a difficult time handling others' comments about your appearance, even if they are positive?

- **How do you treat yourself?** Do you take time for yourself? Do you nurture your body, mind, spirit, and passions? Do you give yourself the self-care you deserve and act as if YOU matter? In short, do you treat yourself as well as you'd like your ideal partner to treat you with value and understanding?

Also, consider what your body language communicates— even when you're alone! For example, good posture can make you feel more confident. Slow, lethargic movements can bring you down (or be an indication that you already are). Fidgeting can be a sign of nervousness. And, of course, smiling almost always elevates your mood!

So, if you're looking to send yourself some self-love signals, try "flirting" with some positive self-talk and feel-good body language!

Interested is Interesting

Another aspect of flirting that applies to many other situations is *being interested*. This doesn't necessarily mean being interested in someone romantically. (It's noteworthy, though, that we use the word, "interested," when someone is attracted to another person: She's *interested* in him.)

In non-romantic contexts, "interest" could simply mean being interested in what someone is saying—really listening to them, rather than looking distractedly around the room or waiting for your chance to jump in and change the subject.

The ability to really listen and show a genuine interest in another person is one of the greatest gifts we can share with one another. At their core, what people want most is to be seen and heard for who they are—and that is something you can offer anyone at anytime, simply by looking at them and listening to what they say.

You'll be amazed at how grateful people will be simply to have someone see and hear them—to take a genuine interest in their lives. Not only is this a wonderful (and free) gift for the other person, but it also enriches your own life. The ability to step outside of your own mind for even a few minutes can offer a fascinating glimpse into a whole new perspective or realm of experience.

Also, "interest" doesn't have to be in another person. It could mean being interested in a subject—an area of study, a hobby, a career, or something in the world beyond yourself that you find fascinating. Such interests not only enrich your own individual life but make you more interesting to others. The ability to express and convey your passions and fascinations to others can be extremely appealing (as long as you don't become self-absorbed or lapse into jargon or off-putting "shop talk").

Being interested—in others, in hobbies, and in your life—makes you a more interesting person. It's also a great way to enrich your own individual life, feel more passion, and show that your interests matter!

In my own life, I never stop looking for fun and different things to learn: photography, scrapbooking, sports, new kinds of reading and writing, public speaking, shopping, travel, exercise programs...you name it, I love it! The problem is, I want to *perfect* every new thing that I try! This can drive my husband NUTSO, because one thing my family and friends know about me is that I am a "plunge in headfirst kinda gal." This means that I tend to be very enthusiastic about my new endeavors. It also

What are your hobbies and personal interests?

means that I sometimes I hit my head on a rock at the bottom! I can get so tenacious about the learning and the creative process that I sometimes become a bit of an absent-minded professor: all-consumed, to the point where I forget that I have kids, a husband, and a need for bathroom breaks!

I am not asking you to be like me (even though I kind of like this about me, and it ROCKS when I am on a roll), but I am asking you to stop, evaluate your interests, and look for new things to dive into to broaden your horizons.

The Heart of Flirting

Tone of voice, body language, and interests are all important aspects of flirting, they're only the external parts. The most powerful part of flirting is *internal*—your feelings, attitude, and energy.

Can you remember a time when you flirted—and enjoyed it? Did you feel more alive, more animated, more like the person you wanted to be? Did you feel interesting, sexy, playful, or cool? Perhaps this was partly due to the fact that you were receiving someone else's attention. And, let's face it, it *is* flattering to have someone interested in you—especially someone you find attractive or alluring. However, it may have had just as much (or more) to do with *how you felt about yourself.* And chances are, those positive feelings can be summed up in one word:

Confidence

Confidence makes all the difference in flirting—and almost any other situation. What's really being communicated by direct eye contact, a firm handshake, and a relaxed demeanor is the message, "I am confident." On the other hand, staring at your shoes while shuffling across the floor with your hands in your pockets communicates exactly the opposite!

Whether you're looking to get a date, get a job, or live a more loving, fulfilling life, boosting your self-confidence is one of the greatest gifts you can give yourself. Confidence means feeling good about who you are.

Does this make you arrogant or conceited? Not at all! Healthy confidence is the opposite of arrogance—it's telling yourself, "I may not be perfect, but I'm good enough." And this kind of confidence is the perfect foundation of self-love.

Unfortunately, you can't just snap your fingers and feel more confident (can you?), but you can take steps to actively increase your self-confidence in ALL areas of life!

Standing Tall

I have a confession to make: I have not always been really confident. Standing at a whopping 4 foot 10 (well, *almost* 4 foot 10), I have in the past been extremely uncomfortable with my physique. Yes, my compact body was wonderful for gymnastics, but in everyday life my muscular shoulders and arms made me feel less elegant and womanly.

These insecurities came to the surface one day in my high-school speech class. I had just given a speech on gymnastics where I wore my gymnastics uniform and did some flips in front of my class. I was feeling great about myself...until the next speaker (an ex-boyfriend) gave a speech where he compared my arms to Arnold Schwarzenegger's. I left the class in tears, and it took quite a while for the teacher to calm me down. Long after the tears dried, however, the insecurities remained.

I do understand that we all have certain parts of ourselves that we are less than confident about. The goal is to find confidence, even in your areas of weakness, and embrace every part of yourself.

YOUR Turn!

Now that you've considered some key elements of the beginning of a relationship—meeting, flirting, and feeling a spark of interest—think (and write) about how they apply to self-love in your own life!

~ EXERCISES ~

Flirtation, Self-Talk, Self-Image, and Body Language

How can you use the power of flirting...with yourself?

Fill out the chart below, thinking about how you can apply the lessons of flirting in a new (potential) relationship to benefit your budding relationship with yourself! (In column 2, write down examples of flirtatious behavior you've experienced or observed in various areas. Then, in column 3, write down ways you could "flirt" with yourself in each area!) Have fun! Play! Enjoy! After all, that's what flirting is all about!

Behavior	Flirtation with Others	Flirtation with Yourself
Speaking		
Body Language		
Dress		
Attitude		
Movement		
(Other behaviors):		

Your Inner Voice

*If you met someone you were interested in—romantically or otherwise—you'd probably speak nicely to them. Do you pay yourself the same courtesy? What does your inner voice sound like? Is it more encouraging or critical? How can you speak more lovingly (and flirtatiously) to yourself?*_____

_____

_____

_____

_____

Flattery will get you everywhere!

*Just as if you were flirting with someone you felt attracted to, compliment yourself on your appearance and/or any other parts of you. (For "extra credit": After you write down the compliments here, say them aloud while looking in the mirror!)*_____

_____

_____

_____

_____

Self-Treatment

How well do you treat yourself? What could you do differently that would reflect a healthy sense of self-esteem and self-worth?

_____

_____

_____

_____

_____

Your Body Language

*How do you stand, sit, and walk (e.g., good posture, slouched, fidgeting)? What message(s) does your body language send to others—and to yourself?*_____

_____

_____

_____

_____

_____

Positive Nonverbal Cues

*What are some nonverbal cues that you consider positive (e.g., good posture, clear voice, eye contact)? What kind of body movements do you admire or find attractive?*_____

_____

_____

_____

_____

_____

*Which of these (and/or other) positive cues would you like to incorporate more of into your own life—and how/when can you practice these?*_____

_____

_____

_____

_____

Caught on Film!

*A great way to become more aware of your body language is to be videotaped and watch yourself on film. Would you consider trying this? If you do this, what about your body language did you notice? Did anything surprise you?*_____

_____

_____

_____

Additional Nonverbal Communication Exercises

In addition to the awareness exercises above, try the following to hone your nonverbal communication skills and use them to your advantage:

- *Observe people in public places. Without listening to their words, see if you can tell what they're communicating. Can you tell when someone's flirting? Can you gauge their level of interest in the person they're with? Can you guess their relationship to one another?*

- *You can also try the same exercise by watching TV with the volume off (or while watching foreign-language programs without subtitles). Can you follow the plot without hearing/understanding the words? Can you tell the characters' moods? Can you tell which ones are romantically involved (or at least interested)?*

- *When you're alone, try changing your body language (e.g., posture, smiling, speed of movements) to see which changes produce the most positive, enlivening effects. When you are ready, try using this positive-feeling body language in public. How do you feel different (alone or with others)?*

Turning Your Interests into "You're Interesting"

Interests, Hobbies, and Passions

*What are some of your main interests—your passions, hobbies, or other activities that excite you?*_____

_____

_____

_____

_____

_____

Focus on the interest (from your list above) that you feel most passionate about. Describe why you are so passionate about it. Imagine telling someone about it—conveying your passion and maybe even infusing them with it, getting them excited about it as well! _____

_____

_____

_____

_____

_____

How could you bring some of this passion to other areas of your life—including other activities, people, and (especially) yourself?

_____

_____

_____

_____

_____

_____

Building Confidence from the Inside Out...and the Outside In

When have you felt most confident?

What are some situations in your life when you've felt the most confident? Visualize, feel, and mentally/emotionally re-create the scenes, including the location, the year and season, and how you felt.

_____

_____

_____

_____

_____

_____

_____

_____

_____

_____

How can you recapture that feeling and apply it to your life now?

_____

_____

_____

_____

_____

_____

_____

_____

Flip It!

What are some areas in your life where you've felt the least *confident? What would it feel like if you could* flip *it? In other words, what if you could turn your lack of confidence into extreme confidence? Fill in the chart below:*

Area in which You've Lacked Confidence	How You've Felt in Those Areas	Flip It! (Describe the Opposite)

Re-imagine one (or more) of the areas above as if you now possess the opposite (from column 3). How might those areas/scenes play out with this extreme confidence? _____

_____

_____

_____

_____

Confidence Role Models

Who are some role models (or anyone else) that you've observed who seem extremely confident—either in general or in specific situations? _____

_____

_____

_____

_____

Borrowing Confidence

Can you imagine yourself in their shoes and "borrow" some of their confidence to use in your own life? Picture a scene from your near future in which you'd like to feel more confident, imagining that you have all the confidence of the people you mentioned above— including yourself at your most confident (or in the imagined "flip- it" exercise). What do you say? How do you act? How do you feel? __

_____

_____

_____

_____

_____

_____

Taking it to the next level...

As Humphrey Bogart said, "I think this is the beginning of a beautiful friendship...with yourself!" OK, so I added that last part, but it's true! By completing this chapter and reflecting on the questions and concepts above, you've laid the groundwork for a beautiful relationship with the person you're closest to: yourself!

But let's not stop here—let's pursue this relationship, just as someone might do with a romantic interest. Now that you've felt a spark of potential and fanned it with a bit of confident flirting, you're ready to take the next step: *dating*.

Chapter Two

Dating

~ *Getting Serious...with Yourself* ~

R ight from the start, I thought that Rick seemed extremely fun, thoughtful, and good-looking; but he wasn't exactly my physical type—I'd always imagined myself with a short, muscular athlete, whereas Rick was 6' 2" and not particularly athletic. As I'd later learn, I wasn't exactly his type either. He'd always thought that he'd end up with a tall, long-legged brunette. I, however, have curly reddish hair and (as I mentioned earlier) stand at a whopping 4' 9½"!

Seeing us together is sort of like seeing a giraffe married to a kitten—an arrangement that has its pros and cons. On the downside, I now have a permanent neck crick from our conversations, and when we slow dance, people think I'm his young daughter. On the brighter side, I have a lifelong partner to help me out with the cabinets higher than 5 feet, and he has somebody to get things off the ground for him. Life and fate can certainly be funny!

Nonetheless, although I was a far cry from the leggy brunette of his fantasies, something about me attracted Rick's interest. I'm not sure if it was my initial shyness, our playfulness together, or my quirky style of dress (let's just say that my fashion sense back in school was a bit...odd), but something made me attractive in his eyes.

After our silly interaction at the "Bowlin Alley" (which had seemed like innocent play to me), Rick tried for months to get me to go out with him. But I just wasn't ready. I'd recently gotten out of a serious relationship, which had shattered my confidence, left me in pain and turmoil, and obliterated my trust in men. I had absolutely no desire to share my innermost self in any sort of intimate way. I figured I'd hunker down and focus on personal growth and medical school.

After many months, however, I finally agreed to go on a date with Rick. He took me to a loud, smoky music hall, which was hosting a "battle of the bands" competition. Despite the noise, we somehow managed to have an enthralling conversation—talking for hours about our lives, philosophies, and worldviews. It was a game of verbal badminton, where as soon as one question was answered, another was immediately shot back. The hours flew by, and I even stopped noticing the blaring "battle" of music!

Despite the stimulating conversation and wonderful connection, however, I still didn't feel ready to jump into a new relationship. So when he brought me back home to my apartment and tried to kiss me, I turned my head so that he only kissed my cheek. This was the beginning of a cat-and-mouse game of Ricky's pursuit and Julia's skittering away.

The turning point came on the night before my first exam in neuroanatomy (the study of the nervous system). Rick had been tutoring me, and we found that we were a perfect match academically, with perfectly reciprocal strengths and challenges. Throughout the semester, this became a wonderfully helpful study arrangement—until the night before the big exam. I'm not sure why I chose that exact moment to finally give in and kiss him, but once I did, months of pent-up frustration came pouring out of us both.

Despite having a wonderful tutor (or perhaps because of it), I barely passed the neuroanatomy exam! My brain was in the classroom, but my mind must have been elsewhere!

Peeling the Onion

Even if you're not studying the nervous system, dating can be a time of nervousness in any budding romantic relationship! It can also be a time of excitement, hopes (and possible disappointments), exploration, fantasies, and fun! It's a time between the initial spark and the seriousness of engagement. It's a time of getting to know someone—and them getting to know you, which means revealing more and more of yourself, much like you would peel the layers of an onion, starting with the outer skin and moving in toward the core.

Know Thyself

Whether you're in a relationship with someone else or just want to get to know *yourself* better, the journey of self-exploration and self-revelation is perhaps the most important and exciting one you'll take in your entire lifetime! Although it's serious, it doesn't have to be a heavy or ominous task. It can be fun—just like dating!

> ## Self-Exploration
>
> *The journey of self-exploration and self-revelation is perhaps the most important and exciting one you'll take in your entire lifetime!*

So, let's use dating as a model while you get to know yourself better than ever—exploring aspects of yourself that often remain hidden or underappreciated, and possibly revealing some pleasant surprises!

But before we explore the deep, inner parts of your being, let's look at the outer layers—starting with your appearance.

Judging a Book by Its Cover

For better or worse, appearances *do* matter.

We've all heard the saying, "You can't judge a book by its cover," but we all do it! We make judgments based on appearance, and especially based on first impressions. And this isn't necessarily a bad thing!

A person's appearance can say a lot about them: Are they a fastidious dresser, or do they look like they just rolled out of bed? Do they exude health and vitality or sickness and depression? Does their aura and appearance invite you in or push you away? And let's not forget body language: the smile or scowl, good posture or slouch, and all of the other physical details that people notice immediately.

This is not to say that we should judge someone as "good" or "bad" based on the way they look. After all, everyone dresses casually on some occasions and gets spruced up for others—and that doesn't change the essence of who they are. But there's no discounting the importance of appearances and first impressions, and nowhere is this more evident than in the world of dating.

Primp and Circumstance

Before you go out on a date—especially a first date—you're likely to primp, to make yourself look as good as you can for the special occasion. Presumably, the date is with someone you're interested in, someone you'd like to make a good impression on. You want to put your best foot (and face) forward.

The same holds true for other important occasions, such as job interviews, when you want to make a good first impression. Again, this is not necessarily a bad thing. (After all, if you were the boss, deciding who to hire between two equally qualified candidates, would you choose the meticulous dresser or the one with the one with mismatched socks?)

While appearance is only one small part of who you are, it can say a lot about you—sending a positive message or raising concerns (e.g., if someone didn't notice their mismatched socks, what else aren't they noticing?). And while deeper aspects of someone's personality are revealed over time, when you first meet, appearance is the only thing you have to go on.

More importantly, this phenomenon works both ways: Not only does your appearance convey messages to others about who you are, but it reflects and affects the way you see yourself! (Do you feel more confident wearing clothes with stains and holes, or a sharp, stylish outfit?) Whether you're going out on a first date, a job interview, or grocery shopping, your appearance can affect your confidence, your self-image, and your sense of self-worth.

This is not to say that everyone needs to look like a fashion model or that there is a "right," one-size-fits-all way that we should look. What is important, however, is that your appearance makes you feel confident and comfortable.

Even if you dismiss appearances as "superficial," people will still make assumptions based on the way you look—they *will* judge a book by its cover! (And, whether you admit it or not, I guarantee that you do the same to others!)

So, whether you're on a literal date, out with friends, or all alone, ask yourself: what message does your appearance send— to others and to yourself? How does it affect how you feel about yourself? What does it say about who you are? Does your appearance feel more like a mask or a reflection of your true self?

And who exactly is your true self anyway?

Who Am I?

There's certainly nothing wrong with looking good and having a good time! It's great to feel confident, have fun, enjoy your life, and enjoy yourself! But dating (like all of life) is more than this—it's also about getting to know someone. And in this book, that "someone" is YOU!

So, at this point in your TMITW journey, you'll address one of the most fundamental questions of life: *Who am I?*

This includes all your experiences, likes and dislikes, skills and talents, weaknesses and challenges, and everything else that goes into making you the person you are. This also includes the hidden parts of yourself that have yet to emerge—not just who you've been and who you are now, but also you are becoming and who you *may* become: your vision, your hopes and dreams, your potential.

You'll delve into all of this and more as you continue the never-ending journey of self-exploration! But for now, we'll proceed along the lines of your budding "romantic" relationship with yourself and take the next step...

The First Date

Imagine that you're going on a first date.

You met someone who sparked your interest, you flirted a bit, and you finally worked up the nerve to ask them on a date—and they accepted!

Before going out, you primp and get dressed in a way that reflects your style and who you really are. When you arrive at the date and see the person, you feel that same jittery excitement, like when you first met. But you also feel confident—and your voice and body language reflect that.

You know it's just the first date, but you have a good feeling about this person. Despite some rocky relationships in your past, you think that this one might actually work out. So you want to start off on a good note. You want to show yourself in a positive light while still being 100% honest and authentic. You want to open up and share who you really are.

But that means that you have to know yourself:

Who are you?

This is a surprisingly profound question, isn't it? After all, there are so many different sides to you: your personality, your thoughts and feelings, and how you act in different situations. The question of identity encompasses *everything* about you—from your past experiences to your goals for the future, from your physical appearance to your innermost spiritual being...and everything in between.

But we won't get too heavy since, after all, this is just the first date! Getting to know yourself—or anyone else—is a gradual process. Start with some of the basics: your likes and dislikes, your upbringing and family life, and what's most important to

---

Your First You-Date

Imagine that you're sitting across a dinner table from a wonderful, intriguing person: YOU!

You want to share some of the things that make you the magnificent, unique individual you are.

What would you say?

How would you show who you truly are?

---

you right now. Consider how each of these reflects—or doesn't reflect—the person you are and the person you'd like to become.

Just like me, you may need to take some time to come out of your shell and be comfortable in conversation—even within your own mind. You may not feel ready to date or even comfortable getting physically and emotionally close with yourself. You may actually turn your proverbial cheek at the goodnight kiss. But remember, this book is about pushing your limits, understanding yourself better, and taking chances.

So, who is this "mysterious stranger" you're with? Are you willing to start peeling back the layers and seeing what (and who) is inside?

The Space Within

"Who am I?" is a deep enough question even when you're alone. But it becomes even more complex once you start interacting with other people or situations—all of which change you, uncover hidden strengths of weaknesses, and reveal new sides of your personality.

Whether it's through dating or other types of relationships, the moment you start interacting with a person, place, or activity you become a different person. You're affected. Different parts of you come to the forefront. Parts of you that have been sleeping start to wake up. And new parts develop.

And as a relationship develops—including the relationship with yourself—you become bigger, richer, more complex. Your life becomes fuller.

You change. You grow. You expand.

You become more you!

One of the most powerful parts of dating—or any relationship—is how it affects and reveals the individuals involved.

There are some relationships that bring out the best in you, and others that seem to bring out your worst. Have you ever been in a relationship with someone who constantly made you angry and put your guard up? Someone who caused you to say things that you never thought you would speak out loud? Someone who brought up feelings of insecurity and imperfection?

On the other hand, you also may have dated someone who brought out your passionate side, or another person who you found intellectually stimulating and helped reveal your own hidden depths. Perhaps you've been in relationships that helped nurture previously latent talents—or others that helped you tap into creativity beyond anything you knew you had.

And this isn't just true with romantic relationships. You probably have some friends who you can relax and be silly with, and others who tend to bring out a more serious side of you. Likewise, certain jobs or other situations bring out one side of you (e.g., more cerebral, physical, organized, or any other quality that the job/situation calls for).

In short, there's far more to you than meets the eye. Sometimes it just takes someone or something outside of yourself to bring those parts to the forefront. This doesn't mean, however, that you're incomplete on your own. Alone, in a relationship, or in any other situation, you are always enough—you are *whole*!

You DON'T Complete Me!

The old model of a relationship was that of two incomplete people looking for their missing piece—the one who would complete them, the "better half" who would make them whole.

More and more, however, people are realizing the importance of coming into a relationship as a whole person. This doesn't mean you aren't nourished by sharing parts of your life with others; it just means that you don't necessarily *need* another person in order to be whole. You can be strong, whole, and independent (rather than needy) alone or within a relationship. *You can be your own better half!*

Rather than weakening relationships, this approach actually strengthens them. Each person has more to offer one another, themselves, and the relationship.

Consider these two overlapping circles:

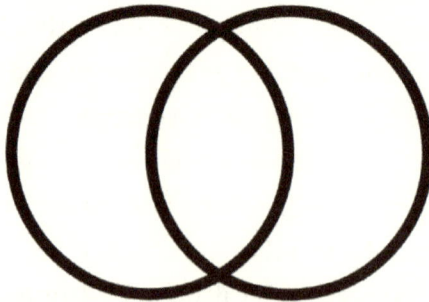

Imagine that each circle represents a whole person in a relationship. The overlapping portion (shaded in below) represents the relationship itself—the intersection where the two people come together.

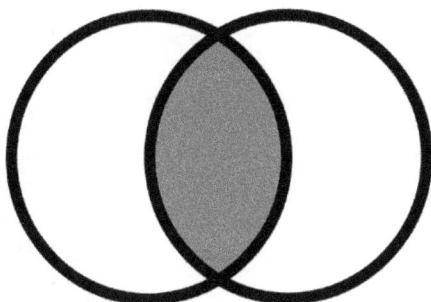

But life is even more complex than that, because you don't only have one relationship—you have many!

- **You have a relationship with every person in your life:** your partner, your friends, your family, your co-workers, and everyone you come in contact with.

- **You also have a relationship with all the activities in your life:** your job, your hobbies, your recreational activities, and anything that you do on a regular basis.

- **And, of course, you have a relationship with yourself**—aside from all of the external people and things in your life.

And all these different parts of your life bring out different parts of YOU.

You can visualize this complex web of life like many interlocking circles—with you in the center:

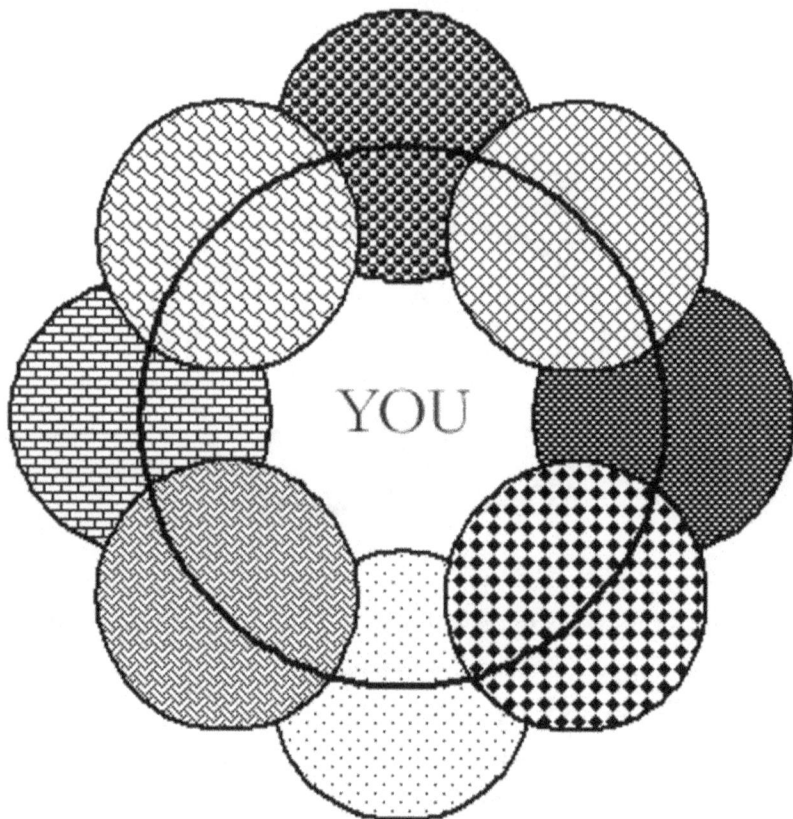

Each smaller circle represents a person, thing, or activity that you have a relationship with—someone or something that affects your life, that affects *you*. All the people and things you relate to have their own patterns and styles. Through your relationships, those patterns enter your own life (overlapping into the center circle). They affect you, change you, bring out different aspects of who you are. They expand you and make you a fuller person with a richer life.

But there is always a part in the very center—the space within all those external influences and relationships, a part that is untouched and unchanged, a part that is just you.

The true you is not just the sum of the relationships you have. Nor is it merely the part that is just you. You are *all* of this—and so much more.

The Representative's Mask

So, with all your relationships bringing out different parts of yourself, how do you know who is the "real you"? Who is your true self, and who is you playing a role?

As comedian Chris Rock has joked, when you meet someone, they're not really meeting *you*—they're meeting your "representative"! This isn't just true for the dating world. We all have many representatives—many masks that we wear in different settings:

- **The Professional** – at work
- **The Good Parent** – with the kids
- **Life of the Party** – out on the town
- **The Dutiful Daughter or Son** – with parents
- **The Seductress (or Stud)** – with lovers

...and dozens of other subpersonalities that show up under different circumstances. And there's absolutely nothing wrong with this! It would probably be very inappropriate to break into song and dance in the middle of the office on a Monday morning, but it would be equally inappropriate to update your account spreadsheets in the middle of a dance club on a Saturday night! Likewise, you might tell your best friend your deepest, darkest secrets; but revealing them to someone you just met two minutes ago would probably not go over very well.

It is totally natural that the representative who shows up for a first date is only a sliver of your full self—representing your most appealing qualities, keeping it positive, and keeping it on the lighter side. Revealing disturbing sides of your past (or present) personality and experiences would probably send most potential mates running for the hills. Yes, everyone has a shadow side, but it's not the side we generally lead with—or parade around in professional settings.

A mask can sometimes be a false self—a deceitful disguise of your true self. More often than not, however, it's merely a partial exposure of your *incomplete* self. It's just a small sliver of the full you. Yes, you can be serious and professional, but you can also cut loose at a party. Yes, you're generally lighthearted and jovial, but you might also be given to occasional bouts of depression.

Human personalities aren't usually "either/or" but, rather, "yes/and"—you're a "solid rock" who also doubts yourself, a passionate (and possibly promiscuous) lover and also a devout church-goer, an honest person who occasionally bends the truth. Human beings are complex creatures! Thousands of apparent contradictions co-exist within each of us.

And while playing so many different roles can leave you feeling divided, you know that throughout it all, you are a single, authentic, whole person—even if no one else sees the entire coalescent picture.

Your new date might only see the brightly colored masks, but you know that there is much more to who you are. You are a full, rich, complicated assortment of roles, personalities, subpersonalities, contradictions, fluctuations, inconsistencies, and beauty—a rich, gorgeous, grotesque, brilliant tapestry woven into a single human fabric.

To know the fullness of your being requires that you look at each of your masks—as well as the person beneath them! Start by identifying the roles that your "representative" plays in different situations, then see who's underneath all of these masks!

Removing Your Masks

There's nothing wrong with actively playing different roles in different situations. In the dating world, for instance, it's generally advisable to wear a positive mask during your first few dates. Eventually, however, you will probably long to expose a fuller portrait of yourself. You will want to be seen as more than one-dimensional (e.g., more than just an efficient worker, a party girl, or a supportive friend). You will want to show up as more than just a representative.

You will want to be a full human being.

And this means showing more than one mask—and then removing them—which can be scary. Removing your masks can make you feel vulnerable. It can expose your weaknesses (or, at least, *perceived* weaknesses). It exposes frailty. It exposes humanity.

And this comes with risk: You risk disappointing people—or confusing them. You risk being ridiculed. You risk rejection.

But you also open yourself up for rewards: closeness, authenticity, and the relief that comes from exposure. You also open yourself up to love. (There's a saying: "We like people for their strength, but we love them for their weakness"—in other words, for their humanity, their *realness*.) We learn to understand their potential human frailty.

Still, this process can be scary, particularly when dating. If you've got a good thing going with someone, you don't want to scare them off with an unflattering revelation. You don't want to blow it! However, you can't love someone you don't know. And you can't know someone you can't see. So if you don't let someone see the true, full person under your masks, there's no way that they can truly love you.

The mask can become a wall that both protects you and imprisons you. The only way to break free is to remove this barrier.

Bringing it back to YOU

Before you remove your masks for others, however, *you'll* want to know for *yourself* exactly who's under there! So, now that you've considered the various masks you wear, take some time to remove those masks—and see who's underneath.

And remember to have fun—just like you would on dates with an alluring romantic interest! Enjoy the process of getting to know yourself better, peeling back the layers, and seeing who's underneath! Just like peeling an onion, we'll start from the outside (appearances and externals) and work our way in toward your true core.

~ EXERCISES ~

Appearances and First Impressions

Style

How would you describe your personal style—including how you dress, your grooming and make-up, and other factors that contribute to your appearance? (Are you suave and debonair? Casual and relaxed? Do you tend to look more like a successful business-person or a beach bum? Remember, no answers or appearances are better than others. This is just a chance to become more aware of your appearance and the effect it might have on others and, more importantly, on you!) _____

_____

_____

_____

_____

What does your overall appearance/style say about you? _____

_____

_____

_____

_____

What do you want *it to say?* _____

_____

_____

_____

_____

First Impressions

When people see you for the first time, what conclusions do you think they might make (rightly or wrongly)? What have you been told about your appearance—by your parents, friends, or others?

_____

_____

_____

_____

In what ways are these impressions/conclusions accurate?

_____

_____

_____

_____

In what ways are they inaccurate? _____

_____

_____

_____

Getting to Know You

Hi! I'm...

How would you introduce yourself to someone you were interested in (after giving your name)? _____

_____

_____

_____

_____

Favorites

What are some of your favorites—books/authors, movies, songs/musicians, or anyone/anything else that's important to you? How do (or don't) they reflect who you are?

_____

_____

_____

_____

_____

What's one of your favorite memories, and how did it shape you?

_____

_____

_____

_____

Digging Deeper: Personality, Talents, Challenges, and Dreams

*What do you consider your most positive trait or characteristic? Why? How/when does it show up in your life?*_____

_____

_____

_____

_____

*What skill, talent, or accomplishment are you most proud of? When have you displayed or experienced it?*_____

_____

_____

_____

_____

What do you consider your greatest challenge? _____

_____

_____

_____

_____

What's your vision of an ideal future? _____

_____

_____

_____

_____

"EXTRA CREDIT": A TMITW You-Date

Go on an actual date—with yourself! Treat yourself to some me-time in a way that nourishes you:

- *Spend some time in a café with a journal or a favorite book.*

- *Go to a movie on your own (especially if it's in a genre that your partner or friends don't like).*

- *Take a solo walk in nature.*

- *...or do any other activity (or non-activity) that nourishes you, stimulates you, and engages your passion for life.*

Hopefully, you'll enjoy these "self-dates" enough to make them a regular part of your life—just like you would have regular outings with someone you were dating. Whatever form they take, the important thing is that you show up for yourself, just as you would for another person who you were interested in.

~~~~~~

Your Representative's Masks

Meet My Representative

*How would you describe your "representative"—the person you generally are when you meet someone for the first time?*_____

_____

_____

_____

_____

_____

What different "masks" do you wear while playing different roles in different situations?

On a first meeting and date: _____

_____

_____

_____

*At home:*_____

_____

_____

_____

At a grocery store or shopping mall: _____

_____

_____

_____

With friends: _____

_____

_____

_____

With family: _____

_____

_____

_____

With a partner/spouse/lover: _____

_____

_____

_____

By yourself: _____

_____

_____

_____

Which one is YOU?

Of your various masks, which are the closest and the furthest from your "true" self? How? _____

_____

_____

_____

_____

_____

_____

_____

Unmasking Yourself

Complete the following sentences:

*People who don't know me well would be very surprised if they knew that I...*_____

_____

_____

I worry that people wouldn't like me if they knew this about me:

_____

_____

_____

On the other hand, I think that many people would LOVE me if they knew this about me: _____

_____

_____

*When I remove all of my masks—when I'm not playing any roles or games or trying to impress anyone—this is what I look like, this is WHO I TRULY AM:*_____

_____

_____

*What about this person am I most embarrassed and/or ashamed of? (In other words, why don't I reveal this side of myself more readily?)*_____

_____

_____

*What about this person do I like and respect the most?*_____

_____

_____

_____

And now for the million-dollar question:
*Can I LOVE this person under the mask—"warts and all"?*_____

The Next Level

Once your masks have been removed—once you have revealed the person underneath the roles and representatives—only then can you see your true self. And only when you truly see yourself can you take your "relationship" to the next level: *love*.

Chapter Three

Love and Engagement

~ Getting Actively Engaged with Your Life ~

L et me ask you three questions: What's your favorite movie that you've *never* seen? What's the best song that you've *never* heard? What food do you *really love*, but have never eaten?

Confused? Good—you should be! These are intentionally ridiculous questions! You can't love a movie you've never seen, a song you've never heard, or a food you've never eaten. Why? Because you haven't experienced them, so you can't *know* them.

Likewise, you have to know a person to love them—and that includes yourself! That's why we started with exercises on "Getting to Know You" and "Unmasking Yourself"—to know yourself, inside and out, so that you can learn to love yourself inside and out!

But what does it really mean—to love yourself (or anyone else, for that matter)? What happens when you feel love? What

What is Love?

Traditional Love
a profoundly tender, passionate affection for another person; desire; extreme liking

TMITW Love
affection and care for yourself; valuing your own welfare and well-being; possessing healthy self-esteem; valuing yourself and your life

do you do with love? Or do you not have to *do* anything other than simply feel it?

The choice is yours.

Finding Love, Nurturing Love

Remember the earlier section on "Response-ability"? Just like you have the ability to respond (or not respond) however you want when you feel a spark, you also choose how to respond when you experience love—for anyone or anything (including yourself!).

Imagine that you've found a small, beautiful flower bud. What are your possible responses? You could walk away and ignore it, you could step on it, or you could nurture it. If you decide to nurture it, there's still no guarantee that it will grow and bloom as you'd hoped, but at least you'd know that you did what you could. (And you'll never know if you don't try—you might always wonder: *what if...?*)

The same is true with love of any kind—romantic, friendship, and even the love of yourself. Just like that flower bud or a romantic interest, YOU have the potential to grow, bloom, and experience a tremendous love within yourself—with or without a romantic partner! You have the potential to feel excitement, nurturance, support, unconditional love, and even romance that doesn't depend on a husband, wife, soul mate, dream lover, best friend, or anyone else. You have the power to experience the closest form of love imaginable: *the love within.*

This love may flourish and blossom on its own, or it may require a little TLC (especially if self-love doesn't come naturally to you, as is the case with so many of us). Sometimes you experience self-love in full bloom, and sometimes it starts as a tiny seed that needs to be nurtured. But while you probably know how to nurture a seed (with water, soil, sunlight, and maybe some fertilizer), how do you nurture self-love?

Nurturing Self-Love

There's no sure-fire formula that will make you love yourself, but there are a number of ways that you can encourage and nurture your seed of self-love. The good news is that you've already taken some of the most important steps:

- **Being open to self-love** – Just by opening this book, you've demonstrated that you are, at the very least, open to the possibility of experiencing self-love.

- **Setting an intention to feel self-love** – Being open to self-love (or anything else) is a great start. But beyond the initial openness ("flirting" with the possibility) and even the desire for self-love comes the *intention* to experience it. If you fully expect and intend to feel more self-love, you're halfway there—or more! (And I assume that you wouldn't bother reading this book if you didn't truly expect and intend to get at least some positive results—in the form of more self-love!)

- **Acting out of self-love** – By doing any of this book's exercises—such as going on "me-time" dates, taking steps to build up your self-confidence, or just getting to know yourself better—you are experiencing self-love in action. (Even if you don't feel it, sometimes just acting as if you did is the first step toward experiencing self-love.)

But what if, despite your best efforts and actions, you're still not having the inner experience of self-love? What if you just don't feel lovable—or never did?

You Deserve Love

As a child, you may have received negative messages—from family, teachers, peers, or even strangers. Perhaps you were repeatedly told that you weren't smart, weren't pretty, would never amount to anything, or that you were bad. Or maybe you received mostly positive messages, but a one-time negative remark really stuck with you—such as my ex-boyfriend's unflattering Schwarzenegger comparison!

As sad as these messages are, what's saddest of all is when you internalize them. As a rational adult, you can consciously reject such messages, but as a child you often accept them unquestioningly. These poisonous beliefs can sink into your psyche. They program your subconscious mind and become a part of your mental/emotional fabric. They color the way you see the world and the way you see yourself. And, in the saddest of all cases, they might make you believe the ultimate lie: that you are not lovable.

The truth, however, is exactly the opposite: *You are infinitely lovable! You deserve love! You ARE love!*

Of course, it's one thing to say this and quite another to believe it—not just on a rational level, but on a deep level, in your gut, at the very core of your being. If you don't already feel, deep down, that you are lovable, how do you start to believe this? How do you gain self-confidence? How do you start to believe in yourself, your inherent worth, and the fact that you deserve unconditional love?

Unconditional Love

There are many ways to nurture self-love, including some of the steps mentioned above:

- being open to the possibility,
- setting an intention, and
- acting *as if* you already feel as much self-love as you'd like to.

In the chapters to come, we will also touch upon many other ways to build on these steps—including a self-love ceremony, finding evidence of your positive qualities and abilities, and renewing your vows to love yourself.

As you go through this process, however, it's important to remember one central truth: *Unconditional love needs no reason!* By its very definition, "unconditional love" is love without conditions—no strings attached! You can simply love yourself because you are worthy of love. You deserve love. You *are* love.

You don't need to prove this. You don't need evidence to validate your lovability. You don't need achievements or accomplishments to earn anyone's love—including your own.

Trying to earn someone's love (especially a parent's love, even if they are deceased) through externals is a futile and misguided effort. With each new achievement, the "goalposts" of love will keep moving back, just out of reach. You will forever be striving after something that is unattainable—because you already have it!

You just have to realize that the love you desire, seek, and strive for is ALREADY within you! Searching for self-love is like running frantically throughout your house, going from room to room trying to find a pair of glasses that's sitting on top of your head! The harder you look, the more frustrated you're likely to become! On the other hand, if you just take a moment to realize what you already have, you will find that you already have access to all the love you could ever want or need!

> ### *You already have access to all the love you could ever want or need!*

Commitment

As a romantic relationship develops, there usually comes a point at which the couple has to decide whether or not they want to commit to one another, to the relationship, to their love.

Few words in our language carry such weight as "commitment"—inspiring strength, confidence, dread, or all of this and more! But what exactly does "commitment" mean?

To commit to someone (or something) means to pledge yourself, to express your intentions, or to give your assurance (as in "I commit to finishing this job"). It can mean to bind or obligate. It can also mean to entrust (as in "to commit your life to God"). At its heart, a commitment is a promise.

Is this a promise you're willing to make to yourself?

The Pros and Cons of Commitment

The good news about making a commitment is that it can make you feel locked in—fully focused, engaged, and empowered.

The *bad* news about making a commitment is that...it can make you feel locked in—trapped, ensnared, enslaved.

Let's explore the value of commitment as well as its limitations. What is the true value of "sticking with it" through it all—the good and the bad, richer and poorer, in sickness and in health? Why would you want to commit to yourself—or anyone or anything else?

The Value of Commitment

Romantic relationships often improve dramatically when both partners have "both feet in"—that is, when they're fully committed. Committing wholeheartedly—and knowing that your partner is also fully committed—can significantly reduce jealousy and second-guessing. It tells your partner that they are worthy of your full love. It shows them that you are serious about them. It sends a message that you intend to make this relationship work—an intention which often becomes a self-fulfilling prophecy.

It's not just in romance or other external relationships that commitment is so valuable, however; work, creative projects, and almost all endeavors benefit tremendously from commitment. Mountain climber William Hutchison Murray eloquently expressed this idea (in a famous quote often misattributed to Goethe):

> [T]he moment one definitely commits oneself, then Providence moves too. All sorts of things occur to help one that would never otherwise have occurred. A whole stream of events issues from the decision, raising in one's favour all manner of unforeseen incidents and meetings and material assistance, which no man could have dreamt would have come his way.[2]

It's true! Oftentimes, the moment you commit to something is when everything seems to flow: doors of opportunity open before you, misgivings are replaced by trust, and momentum builds. And as much as this principle holds true in romantic relationships and acts of creation, it is most powerfully relevant when applied to yourself!

When you commit to yourself (and actually follow through on that commitment), you will almost certainly find your life

---

[2] Murray, W.H. *The Scottish Himalayan Expedition* (Dent, 1951).

miraculously transformed. You will understandably build trust within yourself. You will show yourself that you're worth it. You will tell yourself that you matter.

And you'll be right.

The Limits of Commitment

On the other hand, even the most serious commitment should have its limits. Committing to an unfulfilling romantic relationship would be settling below your potential—and you deserve better than that! Committing to a job that doesn't stimulate you is selling yourself short! Committing to a path that doesn't feel right to you isn't honoring your highest self.

If you're uncertain about making commitment, don't be too quick to dismiss it as "cold feet" or "fear of commitment." If you find yourself thinking, "I wonder if there's someone else out there that might be better for me"—maybe that's because there is! Your hesitation to commit might be your intuition trying to keep you safe and steer you in a healthier direction.

And remember, it's a good idea to revisit your commitments periodically. What seemed like the right path at one time might not look so good further down the road.

For instance, if you were steering a ship that was heading straight for an iceberg, would you obstinately refuse to change course? Would you say, "I committed to taking this route, and I'm not going to break that promise just because there's an obstacle in my path." Of course you wouldn't say that—you would change course! Or, if you couldn't change course in time, you'd jump into a lifeboat and save yourself—I hope! It wouldn't do much good for your dying words to be, "I kept my commitment."

When you make a commitment, you do so to the best of your ability, based on all the knowledge of your mind and the wisdom of your heart at that time. However, things change. Circumstances arise unexpectedly. You may discover new information. You may grow, change, and evolve. You may encounter an iceberg.

This is not to say that you jump ship the moment the waters get choppy—or even if an iceberg appears in the distance. You do everything in your power to stay on course when you can, and change course when you need to.

But before you turn the ship around or jump onto a lifeboat—before you break (or revise) a commitment—ask yourself: Am I acting out of healthy self-care or am I just afraid (or plain old *lazy*)? Am I sabotaging an opportunity for growth? Am I being smart or simply obstinate? Am I acting out of the best interest of my highest self?

Overcommitment to Others

Have you ever known a married couple that can't stand each other? Two people who clearly should not be together, but are sticking it out—perhaps "for the kids" or perhaps just because they made a commitment, and they plan on sticking with it, even if it means making one another miserable for the rest of their lives?

Or perhaps you've known someone who has stayed in a committed relationship that was clearly unhealthy—perhaps even abusive. Victims of domestic violence often give their abusers chance after chance after chance—sticking around (or leaving and then going back)—often, tragically, until it is too late.

In the case of domestic violence or similar abuse, it is very clear that the situation overrides any previous commitments made—including marriage. No marriage contract says, "You must stay together, no matter how badly the person abuses you." Almost anyone would advise a friend (or even a complete stranger) to leave an abusive relationship—and contact the police! And, hopefully, they would take precautionary steps to avoid the abuse from being repeated.

Sometimes, commitment can turn into obstinacy—which can, in extreme cases, be deadly. Despite the tremendous value of commitment in many situations, it can be a serious mistake if it's applied to a harmful person. But can you overcommit in your individual life outside of any relationship?

Overcommitment in Your Own Life

Unlike a marriage, you can never leave yourself. You can't jump ship. You can't legally divorce yourself. You can, however, feel divorced from yourself. And you can change what you're committed to.

A simple rule of thumb regarding commitment is to ask: *Is this commitment moving me closer to or further from my ideal self and ideal life?* In short, is it helping me or harming me?

Again, this is not to say that commitments should be relinquished the moment that any degree of pain or discomfort arises. Oftentimes, pushing beyond your comfort zone involves "growing pains," which benefit you in the long run.

A good physical example of this principle can be found in weight-lifting and other forms of exercise:

When you lift weight close to your maximum ability, you tear

> ## *Overcommitted?*
> *Ask yourself:*
> *Is this commitment helping me or is it harming me?*

small fibers in your muscles. You also may experience discomfort or even pain when you push yourself beyond your earlier limits. And after almost any vigorous workout, you're likely to be sore. All these symptoms, however, are short lived—part of the muscular process of tearing down, rebuilding, and growth.

This is very different from experiencing an injury, such as a torn ligament or broken bone. This is a sign that you have pushed too hard or that something has gone wrong in your workout. Physical injuries do not help you to grow. They are painful reminders of the importance of healthy limitations. So, even if you'd previously committed to lifting a certain amount of weight for a certain number of repetitions, you probably need to re-evaluate this commitment if you sense warning signs of injury.

Although some serious injuries cause permanent damage, the body's ability to heal is nothing short of remarkable. Likewise, the heart and spirit are extremely resilient. This doesn't mean, however, that we should invite injury to ourselves—physical, emotional, or any other kind. It means that you should acknowledge some of the really hard lessons in your life that guide you into significant growth, whether mental, emotional or spiritual.

Ditch the Dud!

Yes, some parts of your life that aren't working as well as you'd like *can* be fixed. Sometimes it just takes some persistence to get over a hurdle or through a rough patch. As I said, you shouldn't always "abandon ship" at the first sign of choppy water. However, there may be parts of your life that are beyond saving and just need to be tossed overboard!

Just as you might "ditch the dud" you were dating if he or she mistreated you, you can also ditch any aspect of your own life that's not serving you and seems beyond repair (or simply isn't worth the effort of dealing with an extreme "fixer-upper"). This goes for unsatisfying jobs, relationships (romantic and otherwise), living situations, or habitual activities. This also applies to negative self-talk.

Hopefully, you wouldn't tolerate a would-be lover constantly criticizing and belittling you, putting you down at every other moment. So why would you put up with that voice in your head verbally abusing you? You deserve a zero-tolerance policy with abuse, whether it comes from yourself or anyone else! Sometimes you can reason with these hyper-critical inner voices, and sometimes, like a hopeless dud of a date, you just have to send them packing!

Saying Yes (or No)

So, after considering the pros and cons of commitment and engagement, you will ultimately have to arrive at your own decision: yes or no. Should you accept a proposal of marriage? Should you commit to a new job? Should you commit to raising children? And, most importantly, should you commit to yourself?

Commitment is a weighty decision. Depending on the commitment, it can determine the course of your life. It signifies a promise. So you want to be sure that it's a promise you intend to keep—and one that you actually *want* to keep! (Remember, this is "for better or worse, for richer or poorer, in sickness and in health, 'til death do you part"!) Committing to yourself should be taken every bit as seriously as committing to a marriage.

My Chariot Awaits

Rick and I had been dating for my middle years of medical school—which is quite an accomplishment! Between the heavy workload and irregular schedules, it was hard to find much time to be together. But when we did, it was quality time that felt even more valuable, as we knew that each minute was a precious gift.

Throughout our intermittent dating, we managed to grow extremely close. During numerous lengthy, heartfelt conversations, we also learned that we were remarkably compatible in many major practical areas: family, sexuality, personal dreams and goals, ideas about our perfect house, family skeletons, and career goals.

One day Rick said that he was going to be taking me out to a very nice dinner, so he told me that I should dress up and leave the entire evening open. So I got all gussied up in my nicest clothes, fixed up my hair and makeup, and waited for my knight in shining armor. After a while, I heard an unfamiliar car horn. When I looked out my window, I was excited and shocked to see a white stretch limo and my man in a tuxedo.

My heart was in my throat as Rick assisted me into the limousine and poured us both glasses of champagne. I had never been inside a limo before—and certainly had never felt so cherished and so special in all my life!

I absolutely did not want to forget a single moment of this experience, but my mind was filling up with a million questions: *Was this really happening? Was this actually my boyfriend? What had I done to deserve this?*

Finally, despite my best attempts to push it down, I finally blurted out the one question that kept bubbling up to the surface: "Are you going to propose to me tonight?"

Rick must have prepared himself for this possibility, because he had a very quick answer to my question: "I cannot believe that you are focusing on all the things that I am not doing for you in this moment rather than all the things that I *am* doing for you in this moment."

Well, that shut me up! (But it also taught me a valuable lesson: Live in the present, and appreciate each moment for what it *is*, rather than focusing on what it *isn't*.)

My unanswered question still lingering in the air between us, we arrived at a four-star French restaurant called *La Maisonette*. I was flabbergasted! I had never been to such a beautiful place or eaten such amazing food! I started with a creamy lobster bisque, and I was in heaven from the first bite. For my main course, I had salmon covered in a pastry puff—the definition of bliss!

Unfortunately, as much as I enjoyed the food, my stomach was unaccustomed to such delectable culinary delights. I soon became nauseated and had to run to the bathroom, where I deposited my lovely four-star cuisine into the porcelain God.

After I recovered and made my way back to the table, my tuxedoed boyfriend promptly got down on one knee and popped the question.

In all of my girlhood fantasies about getting engaged, I never once imagined vomiting mere minutes beforehand. I also never imagined everything this moment brought up in Rick: his fear of rejection, his insecurity that I might not surmount my past demons, and his concern about goal discrepancies. That night, in addition to all the romance and chivalry, Rick truly showed me his vulnerable side. But, aside from the emotional intensity and (in-retrospect) humor of the situation, what I remember most was everything that Rick went through to make me feel special— which I certainly did!

(PS: I said *yes!*)

Engagement

Becoming engaged is one of the biggest acts of love and commitment you can make.

When deciding whether or not to become engaged to another person, there are many factors to consider, such as:

- *Do you love them?*

- *Is there physical attraction and chemistry between you?*

- *Do you have compatible values?*

- *Are you in agreement about children (especially whether or not to have them)?*

- *Do you agree on practical decisions (e.g., where you want to live)?*

- *Are you malleable, flexible, and willing to compromise in healthy ways?*

...and many other aspects of your lives that can affect your decision. (Although, as is so often the case, your heart will probably tell you what's right—regardless of any "checklist" of criteria!)

Deciding whether or not to become engaged with *yourself*, however, involves a whole different perspective—starting with the word itself.

What does "engaged" really mean?

The word "engaged" is commonly used to mean "betrothed" or "pledged to be married." Other definitions, however, extend far beyond a literal marriage. The word can also mean "involved" ("deeply engaged in your work") or, in a mechanical sense, "interlocked" ("the two gears were engaged—therefore, when one moved, so did the other"). As a verb, "engaged" can mean "to occupy someone's attention" ("he engaged her in conversation") or "to attract and hold fast" ("the novel engaged her—she found it very engaging").

These definitions are very different in some ways, but they all have one thing in common: *connection.* When two people or things are engaged, they're connected—they're interacting. It might be in a positive sense (such as to engage in business or engage in conversation) or a negative sense (such as to engage in battle or some other conflict).

The Meanings of Engagement

Betrothed
Committed
Employed
Engrossed
Immersed
Interconnected
Interested
Interlocked
Involved
Joined
Occupied
Pledged
Pre-arranged
Secured

...and many other synonyms—all related to forms of CONNECTION.

Are you engaged with your own life?

Whether you're engaged to be married to another person or engaged with your own life, the idea is to be *connected*—to yourself, to others, and to life itself. To be fully engaged means that you are *involved.* You are not checked out. You realize that what you do matters—it affects other people; it impacts the world around you (just as a moving gear affects other engaged gears). You are present and connected to your life, to yourself.

On the other hand, feeling *disengaged* means that you're checked out, numb, or dissociated. It means that you're not involved, separated from your life, disconnected (much like two gears that become disengaged from one another). It means that you're just going through the motions. If you've ever felt this way—or if you feel this way now—you probably realize that this is only half a life at best: living as a shell, disengaged. This is NOT how you want to go through your life! It doesn't feel happy!

So, perhaps now is the time to get engaged (or re-engaged) with yourself!

Getting engaged—with yourself!

When you get engaged to yourself, you start the process of becoming connected to yourself—to your inner source. And when you do this, you are able to connect with others and with the world around you. You are able to be fully present, to live in the now—to be awake to your own life.

When two people become engaged to be married, they express their desire and intention to be connected. You can also do this with yourself. It starts with having a desire: you have to *want* to be connected, to show up for your own life. And then you have to stay present, stay connected. Even when the going gets tough (in sickness and in health). Even when you feel like checking out, pulling away, disengaging—for better or for worse.

Disengaging and Re-engaging

Have you ever been in a relationship where the other person disengaged—pulled away or checked out—when you didn't want them to, when you wanted to be close and connected? They may have had their reasons: maybe they weren't ready to commit, or they were going through a rough time, or their heart just wasn't in it. Regardless of *why* they disengaged, however, it probably felt pretty terrible for *you*, right? You wanted them to be connected to you, to be present and involved in your life. You may have coaxed, pleaded, cajoled, or even nagged them to be more engaged—most likely to no avail. This may have taught you a painful but important lesson: *You can't control another person.*

But you *can* control yourself! This means that you can choose to be engaged in your own life. Or, if you do find yourself disengaged, you can come back to yourself.

Despite our best intentions, we all disengage from time to time—in relationships and in our individual lives. This can be difficult—no matter which side you're on. But the good news is that you can always come back again—and again and again and again...as many times as it takes. And when you do, remember to welcome yourself back—with open arms!

Self-Engaged

Now is your chance to *engage* with this material and with yourself!

Take some time to consider the following questions and exercises, get in touch with your inherent lovability, and think of all the great reasons to commit to yourself and get engaged in your own life!

~ EXERCISES ~

Affirming Your Unconditional Lovability

Negative Messages

Describe a negative message you've received about yourself (especially as a child)—something that made you feel that you didn't deserve love. _____

_____

_____

*Negative messages are an expression of fear. What fear on the part of the speaker was being expressed in the message you described above?*_____

_____

_____

Flip the Fear, and Reinforce the Love!

Recognizing that the message was based on the speaker's fear, as opposed to the deficiency you internalized from it, you are now ready to flip that lie into a truth! Remember the earlier "FLIP-IT" exercise, where you remembered a time when you lacked confidence, then turned that feeling around? Let's do the same thing with the message you wrote above—flip it around and rewrite it so that it reinforces just how lovable you are, and always have been and always will be! _____

_____

_____

What are some other positive statements or affirmations that reinforce the truth that you deserve love? _____

_____

_____

_____

_____

Repeat these affirmations as often as you like—until you feel their truth at the deepest level of your being. And then keep saying them anyway—just like you'd say "I love you" many times to a loved one, even if you both already know it—just because it's always nice to hear!

To Commit or Not to Commit?

Considering Your Commitments

*Who or what in your life are you considering committing to? What about this potential commitment appeals to you? What are your reservations?*_____

_____

_____

_____

_____

_____

If you had to make a decision about this commitment right now—at this very moment—what would you say? Don't think about it—just answer Yes or No: _____

What commitments have you made in the past that are no longer serving you—or perhaps even harming you—in the following areas:

Relationships? _____

_____

_____

*Jobs?*_____

_____

_____

*Financial Commitments?*_____

_____

_____

*Other Commitments?*_____

_____

_____

Make or Break?

What commitments could you make that would most benefit you?

_____

_____

_____

What commitment (s) would it be most beneficial to break or say no to (e.g., work decisions, relationships, financial commitments)?

_____

_____

_____

Are you fully committed to yourself and to living your best life? Do you have "both feet in" in your own life? If not, what would it take for you to feel fully committed to yourself?

_____

_____

_____

Self-Engagement

Feeling Engaged

When have you felt the most engaged in your own life? How old were you? What was going on in your external life (activities, relationships, etc.)? How did you feel? _____

_____

_____

_____

_____

_____

Describe a time when you re-engaged with your life—a time when you'd been disconnected, but came back to yourself, a time when you "got it back" (or rediscovered your "mojo"). How did this happen? What decisions did you make? What plans did you follow through with? What goals did you accomplish? _____

_____

_____

_____

_____

_____

What would have to happen for you to experience something like this now—a significant increase in your level of engagement with your own life? How could you tap into the feelings from earlier engaged times and bring them into your current life? _____

_____

_____

_____

_____

_____

_____

The Benefits of Disengagement

In what areas of your life would you like to DISENGAGE or be less engaged than you currently are? _____

_____

_____

_____

_____

_____

_____

How will you benefit from being less connected (or entirely disconnected) from certain people, activities, or situations? _____

_____

_____

_____

_____

_____

Celebrate Your Engagement

Just as a couple might celebrate their engagement to be married or hold a Commitment Ceremony, you can celebrate your own commitment to yourself. Before you fast-forward ahead to start planning a wedding (and honeymoon...and the rest of your life!) take some time to honor and celebrate your decision to commit to your life—to say YES to yourself right now!

(And *then* you can start picking out the china!)

Chapter Four

Planning and Preparation

~ It's All in the "Me-tails" ~

I had planned out almost every detail of my wedding, but I kept having nightmares that something would go wrong: The flower arrangements would tip over. I wouldn't make it there on time. The groom wouldn't show up on time—or at all! And yes, I even had my own variation of that classic anxiety dream: realizing, right in the middle of saying my vows, that I was stark naked!

My desire for the "perfect" wedding was literally giving me nightmares!

It's very common for people planning weddings to worry (in dreams, as well as in waking life) that something will go wrong. This wasn't entirely unexpected. What I didn't expect, however, was that my anxiety dreams would last for months *after my wedding*—even though the event itself went off without a hitch!

Details and Me-tails

You never realize how much is involved in a wedding until you start planning one. So many variables, decisions, and details go into those few hours:

- vows

- venue

- food

- music

- clothes

- guest list

- decorations

- rings

...and the list goes on and on and on! It can be overwhelming! How do you make all these decisions?

While every individual and couple is different, I believe that there is one guiding principle for all the details that go into planning a wedding:

Let every detail be a reflection of YOU!

If you are very religious, get married in a house of worship. If you are a nature-lover, get married outdoors. Play the music that you love. Serve your favorite foods. If you are formal, use formal decorations. If you are casual, let the setting reflect that. If you are traditional, have a traditional ceremony. If you are creative, make the entire event a work of art!

Me-tails

The same idea holds true for your entire life: Ideally, *every* aspect of your life should reflect who you are—your clothes, your home, your friends, your job, your pets,...everything! Why not let it all be an embodiment of your personality, aesthetic taste, core values, and individuality?

So often, however, we just live by default—not taking the time to make our lives and our surroundings reflect our true selves. It might just seem like too much trouble (or expense), or maybe you have to compromise with a spouse, roommates, or co-workers. Or perhaps you've just gotten so out of the habit of making your life reflect your true self that you've lost touch with yourself altogether—you might even have a hard time thinking of what *would* reflect you!

This is a great opportunity to get back in touch with who you are, what matters to you, and what you love. Imagine that you're planning your ideal wedding—just for yourself—and you want every detail to be a reflection of who you truly are. Where would it be? What colors would you decorate with? What music would you play? What food would you serve? What would embody your style, values, personality, and essence? What would make a guest at your wedding (who *really* knows you well) say, "This is all so...YOU!"?

Make EVERY Day Your Wedding Day!

While you probably couldn't (or wouldn't want to) literally get married every single day of your life, you can incorporate many of the elements and details from your ideal wedding into your daily life.

For instance, if your ideal wedding venue is a beautiful mountaintop—because you love nature—perhaps you can spend more time outdoors on a regular basis.

Color Associations

Qualities, moods, and emotions commonly associated with colors:

- **Red** – love, passion, power
- **Orange** –energy, balance, warmth
- **Green** – nature, health, money
- **Blue** – trust, security, order
- **Purple** – spirituality, mystery, transformation
- **Black** – elegance, sophistication, sexuality
- **White** – purity, cleanliness, innocence

*You'll have your own tastes and associations, so honor your own style! But no matter what colors or other details you'd choose for your ideal wedding, remember to bring them into your life **right now**!*

If your ideal wedding would feature a live jazz band, but you realize you hardly ever listen to jazz anymore, then you might want to make a point of getting out to some jazz clubs—or at least listening to your favorite music on your stereo on a regular basis.

If your ideal wedding colors are bright, warm colors (such as orange, red, and bright yellow), make sure that you decorate your own house with these colors—so you can see them every day, rather than waiting for a special occasion.

Think of all the important aspects of your life, tastes, and personality that you've neglected to nourish, and let your TMITW "wedding planning" serve as a reminder!

The Guest List

Although the decorations and other details (or "me-tails") are certainly important, an even bigger part of your special day is who you share it with—not just the bride or groom, but all the guests! Who would you invite to your ideal wedding?

So many factors go into deciding whom to invite (or not invite) to a wedding:

- **How many people do I want?** A big, grand wedding or a small, intimate wedding—or somewhere in between?

- **How many people can I *afford*?** More meals, larger venues, and other "per-head" expenses can add up fast!

- **Who do I *have to* invite—or at least *feel* like I have to invite?** Family, close family friends, neighbors, and other people who it would be a faux pas—or at least awkward—not to invite.

...and so on. So many considerations: family dynamics, finances, the potential for bruised egos, social/filial obligations, and all the other factors that have nothing to do with the core issue:

Who do you REALLY WANT at your wedding?

Imagine that you didn't have to worry about what *anybody* else thought. Imagine that nobody would be bothered if they were left off the guest list, and everyone you invited would actually attend. And—while we're imagining—let's say that money is absolutely no object.

Who would you most want to share one of the most special, deeply personal moments of your life? This question is for you and you alone to answer, but I encourage you to consider inviting a special group of people: *your champions.*

Who are your champions?

We usually think of "champions" as winners: gold medalists, "champions of the world," and victorious sports heroes. But there's another type of champion: someone who supports or protects you and your desires (as in a "champion of the cause").

So, who are your champions—the people who support and defend you? Who lifts you up? Who's got your back? Who *really* wants you to succeed— and will help you do it?

Your champions could be people you know well—your closest friends and family members. They might be people you don't know extremely well, but who really want to see you succeed (e.g., members of a support group, class, or online community). They might be role models or people who inspire you (e.g., a favorite writer or inspirational speaker—someone who you know would want you to reach your fullest potential).

These are the people who would be wonderful to have around you on your "big day"—or any other day, for that matter! So, think about who would make your list—and then invite them to be a bigger part of your life *right now*!

You Can't Please Everybody

As Bill Cosby famously said, "I don't know the key to success, but the key to failure is trying to please everybody."

Perhaps nowhere is this truer than at a wedding. If you're lucky enough to get a bride and groom who agree on all (or even most of) the details, there are always going to be unhappy parents, bridesmaids, groomsmen, friends, or other guests. One family thinks the ceremony is too religious; another thinks it's not religious enough. Someone doesn't like the food. Another person thinks the music is too loud. And everyone thinks that they should be sitting at the bride and groom's table (even though it only seats eight).

If you can accept that not everyone will always like what you like (or what you do), you will be much happier than if you try to please everyone. And this isn't just for weddings—it's true in every aspect of your life!

This doesn't mean that you should never compromise or take other perspectives into consideration, but remember that *you* are ultimately responsible for your own happiness—just like everyone else is responsible for theirs!

Registering for Gifts

One of the most popular customs of weddings (at least in the U.S.) is the practice of registering for gifts. It's the adult version of a child's letter to Santa: you get to say exactly what you want—with the full expectation that you'll actually get it! What could be more wonderful!

But how does this wedding custom apply to your everyday, individual life? It all boils down to a single word—one of the most important and powerful words in the world:

Ask

Those three little letters change everything. Taking that one simple action—and making a *habit* out of it—may very well be the most important thing you ever do. When you ask for what you want or need, your entire life can be transformed.

Whether asking for a wedding gift, a present from Santa, a promotion at work, a favor from your spouse, directions to a store, or anything else, *clarity is key*. The more clear and specific you can be, the more likely you are to get what you want. A common example of this is typing what you want to search for on Google. For instance, if you want to learn the best way to slice thick cheese, you have to word your question carefully— otherwise, your results may not be about "cutting the cheese" in the way you intended!

In my marriage, years of unwanted Christmas presents have taught me the importance of asking clearly for what I want. For years, my husband went to great lengths (and great expense) to get me "perfect" Christmas presents, until I finally told him it meant more to me for him to give me with things that were more heartfelt than "moneyfelt." The next year, the best Christmas gifts he got me were stocking stuffers of my favorite hand lotion and lip balm. Although they weren't expensive, they showed me that he had paid attention and knew what was important to me—a gift that far outweighed *any* material objects!

(I will, however, add the caveat that you should be careful what you wish for, because you just might get it more than once! This is what happened to me one Christmas when I made a "Dear Santa" list of what I wanted, including a gym bag and a purple purse. Unfortunately, my list got passed around to the whole family, and I ended up with four purple purses and four gym bags that year!)

The practice of asking isn't just for Christmas, weddings, or other special occasions. You can make it a habit in your everyday home life, in business, and any other area of life. Ask for help. Ask for what you want. Speak directly. When you do, you'll see huge results: Doors will open. People will give you what you want—or direct you to others who can (and will). You will develop connections, bonds, and community. And you'll be doing everyone else a favor by not expecting them to read your mind!

Asking isn't just about posing questions to people. In it's broader sense, it's about reaching out and pursuing what you want. For instance, when I wanted to improve my public speaking, I simply Googled "speaking improvement" and was pleasantly surprised to find that one of the largest and most successful Toastmasters clubs was right here in my local town of Greenville, Ohio. By simply "asking" a search engine for what I wanted, I was led toward a more successful professional-speaking career.

More recently, I asked my Facebook friends if they would be willing to help me proofread this book. It was very difficult and awkward for me to ask help (I'm still learning my own lessons!), but many people responded and offered some of the most amazing and helpful feedback. As a result, I believe this book offers much more depth, breadth, and understanding.

Regardless of what you're looking for, when you ask for what you want—clearly and directly—people will respect you. You will respect yourself. You will start seeing yourself as worthy— as deserving of asking for (and getting) what's important to you. You will see your world transform—within you and all around you—as if by magic.

It doesn't hurt to ask.

This isn't only true when you get what you ask for. Even if the answer is "no," at least you won't have to go through your whole life filled with regret, wondering *"What if...?"*. You have nothing to lose by asking, and the worst-case scenario is that you won't have something you already didn't have!

More often than not, however, the answer will be *yes*. You'll be amazed at what a giving world you live in, filled with kind people with generous spirits. Most people are happy to help, happy to give—and happy to be asked, so that they know that the gift is actually desired and appreciated. By asking (and receiving), you're really giving a gift to the prospective giver! You are being a gracious receiver.

Yet many people find it difficult to ask for what they want or need—except when it comes to registering for wedding gifts! This is one of the few times when it's culturally acceptable for an adult to say, "I'd like _____"... and fully expect to get it. You can ask for a set of china, furniture, baby clothes, or anything else that you really want—without feeling any embarrassment.

You're not *forcing* anyone to buy you anything. Of course, people won't buy gifts that are beyond their budgets or go against their values (e.g., a vegetarian probably isn't going to buy you that leather couch you've registered for). And they can always buy gifts that you haven't registered for. So you're not putting anyone in an awkward position. In fact, registering for gifts actually helps the gift givers—especially if they have no idea of what you want or need. They can just go down the registry list and find something that fits into their budget.

Easy!

Non-wedding Registry

What if you took the "registry" approach in all situations—not just weddings?

Just think of how much easier life would be if you were *always* so straightforward and unapologetic about asking for what you want or need. No beating around the bush. No expecting others to read your mind. No sending subtle, coded messages and then feeling disappointed and/or resentful when people don't figure them out. No feeling embarrassed, selfish, or greedy for asking for what you want or need. And no sour grapes—saying, "That's OK—I didn't *really* want it," when you don't get something that you clearly *did* want!

And think of how much easier it would be for the people on the other end: They no longer have to read your mind, decode cryptic signals, or risk disappointing you.

Imagine a world where, when someone wanted something, they simply said, "I would like _____." It wouldn't mean that anyone would be *forced* to give. It would just mean that the desire and request would be out in the open—in clear, unambiguous terms. No more guessing games. No more neon purple sweaters that don't fit, no more out-of-date cheap ties, no more nasty fruitcake!

Aaaaaahhh...what a relief for *everyone*!

You Deserve Help

Even more important than asking for specific gifts is the habit of asking for *help*—whether it's at a wedding or in your everyday life.

Despite this book's focus on individual empowerment, the truth is: a wedding is not a job for one! Even if you planned a wedding alone (or with your spouse-to-be), you would probably still need MANY other people: a best man, bridesmaids, an officiant, and witnesses, as well as a host of other supportive people, such as a chef, caterers, a band and/or DJ, a hairdresser, and anyone/everyone else who helps you with the details of your big day. (Even if you elope, you would still need an officiant and a witness!)

And all this help is wonderful! The help you receive from all these people is one of the greatest wedding gifts you'll get!

When it comes to weddings, most people realize the importance—or necessity—of getting help from others. It's expected. Like registering for gifts, it's socially acceptable to ask for help with weddings. Yet how many people are reluctant to ask for help in other situations?

Perhaps this is because some people see asking for help as a sign of weakness. Perhaps some men don't consider it "manly" to admit that they can't (or simply don't want to) take care of everything alone. Perhaps a woman doesn't want to be seen as a helpless "damsel in distress." Or perhaps you've been raised to value independence—"pulling yourself up by your own bootstraps."

But there's a difference between self-reliance and feeling that you always have to "go it alone" or "carry the weight of the world on your shoulders." The truth is:

Asking for help isn't a sign of weakness—it's a sign of intelligence and assertiveness!

Carrying too much? Ask for help!

Do you ever find yourself wanting help, but not wanting to ask for it—or even turning down offers for help? You might say to yourself or would-be helpers, "It's OK—I've got it. I can do it alone." And yes, you probably *can* do it alone. But that doesn't mean that you *have to* do it alone or that it's in your best interest to do it alone.

Remember: No man (or woman or couple) is an island. You don't have to go it alone! This is the benefit of living in a society.

The truth is that most people enjoy helping—either from the goodness of their hearts or because they get paid for it! Asking for—and graciously receiving—help is a gift that you can give to others. It builds a sense of community, a sense that "we're all in this together"—because we are!

But if you still find yourself reluctant to ask for help, try making this small shift:

Change "I need help" to "I deserve help"!

You DO deserve help! You do more than enough already! You have better things to do with your time! You're worth it!

So, what are some ways that you deserve help? If you're an overworked (and/or overwhelmed) mother, maybe you could hire a housecleaner or get a friend to watch your kids one afternoon a week so that you can have some YOU-time. If you're a man who does all of the yard work, maybe you could hire someone to help and/or ask your partner (or kids or anyone else) to help you. If you're having a tough time emotionally, maybe you could reach out for help from a friend, preacher or minister, counselor, or therapist.

People *want* to help you! They want to feel needed. And—especially if they're your true friends and champions—they want to see you live your best life!

Don't you want that, too?

Inner Preparation: Pre-ME-marital Counseling

With all the planning and preparation that goes into a wedding (and just about every other part of life), you might forget to get ready on the inside. No, I don't mean decorating the venue walls, I mean preparing emotionally.

Just as couples often go to premarital counseling—to make sure that they are prepared for the commitment they're about to make to one another—you can benefit from a similar process as an individual. Some of the questions that arise in premarital counseling demand intense introspection and soul-searching (such as religious beliefs and values). Others may be more a matter of practical preferences (such as where you'd like to live).

If you are going to spend the rest of your life with this person, it is probably a good idea to know them as well as possible. In traditional premarital counseling, this includes learning as much as you can about your partner. In *TMITW* pre-ME-marital counseling, this means learning more about yourself!

So, grab a pen, open your heart, and get ready to learn more about your most intimate life-partner: YOU!

~ EXERCISES ~

Planning the Wedding Details (or "ME-tails")

Describe each detail of your ideal wedding, and explain how it represents YOU!

Ceremony

Description/Details (e.g., formal/casual, religious/secular, time of year, day/night): _____

_____

_____

_____

How this represents YOU: _____

_____

_____

_____

Ceremony Venue

Description/Details (e.g., church/house of worship, outdoors, beach, mountaintop, destination wedding, nearby, or at home): ___

_____

_____

_____

How this represents YOU: _____

_____

_____

_____

Reception
Description/Details (e.g., quiet gathering, raucous party, dancing):

_____

_____

_____

How this represents YOU: _____

_____

_____

_____

Reception Venue
Description/Details (e.g., size, location, style): _____

_____

_____

_____

How this represents YOU: _____

_____

_____

_____

Music
Description/Details (e.g., live band, DJ, rock, pop, jazz, classical):

_____

_____

_____

How this represents YOU: _____

_____

_____

_____

Food

Description/Details (e.g., ethnic cuisine, vegetarian health food or backyard barbeque, formal sit-down meal or casual buffet):

_____

_____

_____

How this represents YOU: _____

_____

_____

Decorations

Description/Details (simple or elaborate, formal or rustic, flowers or hay bales): _____

_____

_____

_____

How this represents YOU: _____

_____

_____

Rings

Description/Details (diamonds, gold, modern, family heirlooms):

_____

_____

_____

How this represents YOU: _____

_____

_____

Vows

Description/Details (traditional, personalized, religious, serious, light-hearted): _____

_____

_____

_____

How this represents YOU: _____

_____

_____

Clothes

Description/Details (e.g., traditional wedding dress, tuxedo, modern, casual, artistic): _____

_____

_____

_____

How this represents YOU: _____

_____

_____

Party Gifts

Description/Details (e.g., small tokens just for wedding party or extravagant gifts for everyone at the wedding): _____

_____

_____

_____

How this represents YOU: _____

_____

_____

Style/Colors

Description/Details (traditional, modern, black and white, vibrant and colorful): _____

_____

_____

_____

How this represents YOU: _____

_____

_____

_____

Other Aspects

Description/Details (e.g., how long, how big, how many speeches, activities, unusual aspects, overall tone): _____

_____

_____

_____

_____

_____

How these represent YOU: _____

_____

_____

_____

_____

_____

~~~~~~
Everyday Wedding "ME-tails"

What are some ways that you can bring elements of your ideal wedding into your everyday life?

Location: _____

_____

_____

Activities: _____

_____

_____

Style/Colors: _____

_____

_____

Clothes: _____

_____

_____

Music: _____

_____

_____

Other Detail(s): _____

_____

_____

_____

~~~~~~

Guest List of Champions

Your personal champions
Make a list of your champions—those who support and uplift you—and say why it would be great to have each of them at your TMITW wedding. _____

_____

_____

_____

_____

_____

_____

(Use additional paper as necessary. Remember, it's YOUR ideal wedding—you can make it as big as you want!)

You don't have to wait until a wedding!
Write ways that you can surround yourself with the people you've listed above—spending more time with those that you'd like to, bringing those who are at a distance closer to you (e.g., connecting directly with someone who you currently admire from afar), and spending a higher percentage of your time interacting with your champions, cheerleaders, and supporters. _____

_____

_____

_____

_____

_____

_____

New Champions

How can you find new champions (e.g., going to see a life coach and/or career counselor, attending self-improvement seminars, joining Toastmasters, taking classes)? _____

_____

_____

_____

_____

_____

_____

_____

_____

Saying Goodbye to Non-Champions

On the flipside, how can you minimize your interactions with people who aren't your champions? How can you shake off the naysayers, saboteurs, and "energy vampires" (people who drain you)? Is there anyone you'd like to distance yourself from (or completely break off contact with)? How can you do this? Or, if you feel that you have to be around certain unsupportive people, how can you shield yourself from their draining energy or change their affect on you? _____

_____

_____

_____

_____

_____

_____

_____

The Price of People-Pleasing

Describe a time when you tried to please everyone else—and ended up making yourself (and/or others) less happy in the process.

_____

_____

_____

_____

In what parts of your life now would you be happier if you didn't try so hard to please everyone else? _____

_____

_____

_____

"Register" for Gifts

Imagine that you're "registering" for gifts—things that you want from others or from the world. Let your imagination soar! Write down physical/tangible items (e.g., "a new car"), actions or services (e.g., "someone to mow my lawn"), or even non-physical gifts (e.g., "respect" or "understanding"). Have fun, and remember: it doesn't hurt to ask! _____

_____

_____

_____

_____

_____

(Use additional paper as necessary. No limits!)

~~~~~~

A Village of Helpers

Have you ever heard the saying, "It takes a village to raise a child"? Well, it also takes a village to raise an adult—or do almost anything else! In the following questions, think of ways that you could benefit from being part of "the village"—and getting help raising your child (inner or outer!) or in any other part of your life.

*What are some areas in which you would like—and could benefit from—getting help (e.g., getting motivated, dietary or exercise help/training, cooking classes, legal aid, career and educational direction)?*_____

_____

_____

_____

*If you had to pick one item from the list above that you would most welcome, what would it be? What step(s) could you take to actually get this help?*_____

_____

_____

_____

*If you did get all of the help you want (and deserve), what are some things you might enjoy doing with the time and energy that getting help saved you?*_____

_____

_____

_____

〜〜〜〜〜〜〜〜〜〜〜〜〜〜〜〜〜〜〜〜〜〜〜〜〜〜〜〜〜〜〜〜〜〜

Pre-ME-marital Counseling

The following are some questions and issues that frequently arise during premarital counseling sessions—and some that I've inserted just for you! Consider them with regard to your own individual life. Even if you already know the answers, it can help to clarify your thoughts and feelings about important areas of your life. And you never know—you may even surprise yourself with what comes out!

"What You Should Know About Me"

*Imagine that you are about to get married. What are some things that you think your spouse-to-be should know about you? They can be quirks and idiosyncrasies (e.g., I can't stand overhead lights, I like cheese on my apple pie), physical (e.g., I have sticky, sweaty feet), behavioral (e.g., when I get home, I like to take a few minutes to settle in before I start talking or diving into some new activity), or deep and emotional (e.g., when I'm upset, I like to take some time on my own. That doesn't mean that I'm pulling away; it just means that I need to get clear within myself before I try to communicate with someone else, so give me space and I promise to come back to you when I'm ready).*_____

_____

_____

_____

_____

_____

_____

_____

*What is your definition of love (including self-love)?*_____

_____

_____

_____

_____

Family

Summarize the overall dynamic of the family you grew up in and explain how you fit in (e.g., were you the rebel, the peacemaker, or "Daddy's Little Girl"?) _____

_____

_____

_____

_____

Where were you in the sibling lineup, and how did this affect you? (E.g., Were you were the youngest and always treated like a baby; or were you the oldest and expected to be responsible, taking care of younger siblings?) _____

_____

_____

_____

_____

*How did you view your parents when you were growing up versus now that you are an adult?*_____

_____

_____

_____

_____

How does your present life reflect (or differ from) the role you played in your family while growing up? _____

_____

_____

_____

_____

Do you have any children? If yes, how would you describe your parenting style? If no, what type of parent do you think you would be—or would you like to be? _____

_____

_____

_____

_____

Relationships

Describe your parents' relationship: _____

_____

_____

_____

_____

In what ways have your relationships been like or unlike your parents' relationship? _____

_____

_____

_____

_____

Do you see any patterns in your relationships—such as the types of people you've been involved with, the issues that arose, and how you dealt with challenges? (E.g., Did you frequently get into fights caused by jealousy, did the passion die out after 6 months, did you withdraw, did you lack staying power when the newness wore off, or did you stick around long after the relationship was dead?)

_____

_____

_____

_____

_____

_____

*Think about one of your best relationships (current or past). What do you (or did you) like most about yourself when you are/were with this person? How can you embody these qualities more often in other areas of your life?*_____

_____

_____

_____

_____

_____

*What about you would make a potential spouse most lucky to marry you? What makes you a "good catch"?*_____

_____

_____

_____

_____

_____

If you could change yourself in one way, what would it be? _____

_____

_____

_____

_____

_____

And now for another "million-dollar question":
If you DIDN'T change in this way (or in any way), could you still love yourself unconditionally? Could you still honor and cherish yourself for exactly who you are? Would you be ready to commit— really, wholly commit—to yourself forever after? _____

Ready to Take the Plunge!

Now that you've prepared—considered many of the most important external and internal factors that go into a wedding (and a life), gotten in touch with your personal preferences, asked for what you deserve, learned more about yourself, and expressed a desire to commit to yourself—you're ready to "take the plunge"!

You're ready for your big day!

Chapter Five

The Big Day

~ *Tying the Knot with Yourself* ~

My wedding day was absolutely beautiful. The setting was perfect—thanks to my parents and the rest of my family. My family and friends were all there, and even the groom showed up! Despite all my fears, anxieties, and nightmares, the ceremony went without a hitch. All in all, it was that rare wedding where absolutely nothing went wrong.

So why wasn't it the perfect day? What was missing?

In a word: ME!

I wasn't there. Not *really* there. Sure, I was there physically, but I was so nervous that I couldn't relax and enjoy the moment. In fact, I spent most of the day "checked out"—so much so that I actually have memory blanks of the ceremony and reception. And no, I wasn't too drunk—so I can't even use that as an excuse. (Although, I admit, someone in my wedding party did give me a gin and tonic before the ceremony—just enough to calm my nerves...supposedly!)

The parts I remember most were the numerous times I retreated to a locker room just off of the main reception area. I'd go there to hide out on my own or with a few like-minded women looking to escape the noisy, overwhelming throng of the party.

By all accounts, it was a beautiful wedding from beginning to end. Too bad I missed most of it because I was so detached due to nervousness!

This Magic Moment

We all want to be fully present for life's big moments: weddings, graduations, awards, our child's first day of school, and other special occasions. Sometimes it works: we make sure that we soak in every moment—taking mental (or literal) snapshots, savoring every morsel of food, and seemingly stretching every minute into an hour, milking every drop from the experience.

At other times, however, we can psych ourselves up (and out) so much that it backfires: the big moments seem surreal— they blur by, or (like me at my own wedding) we "check out" (or even *black* out!) and miss them altogether. We look back at pictures of the events and feel like we weren't even there.

We often spend so much time planning for the future (especially with weddings) and reminiscing about the past (for instance, looking at wedding photos) that it's easy to miss the one and only time when life actually happens: NOW!

And it's not just the special occasions or "big" moments that are worth showing up for. We want to be present no matter *what* the occasion (or lack thereof). We don't want to miss our lives! Yet somehow, days, months, and even years can go by without us feeling truly present—without feeling like we're really there in our lives, moment to moment. And if you're not really *there*, in your life from moment to moment, you're missing your own "wedding"—and your own life! As the saying goes: "The best present you'll ever receive is the present!" Make sure to graciously receive this gift!

The good news is that regardless of why, how, or for how long you may have checked out, you can always check back in. It only takes a moment.

But how do we come back?

Coming Back to Now

It's natural to drift off, space out, or even check out from time to time. Nobody is 100% present 100% of the time. The key, however, is to keep coming back to the present, the here and now—back to being engaged in your life, back to *you*.

There are many ways to do this, including numerous meditation techniques, mindfulness exercises, and physical reminders. Some techniques use the breath, some use a mantra (a repeated word or phrase), while others use guided imagery. Some people find hypnosis or biofeedback helpful in keeping them grounded in the here and now. And many people like to use everyday life as reminders to come back to the present moment—back to you. (For instance, one technique is to take a deep, centering breath every time you're stopped at a red light. This is a doubly great practice, since it takes a situation that often triggers frustration or irritation and flips it into a positive reminder.)

While many people use a formal practice for extended periods of time each day, I prefer a simple approach that I call "MMM" (for "Many Meditative Moments"). I like to practice this any time I feel myself becoming scattered or overwhelmed or if I start to drift off (although you certainly don't have to wait for a negative feeling to practice this). I simply stop whatever I'm doing, take several deep breaths, and ground myself in the moment. Usually, within a few moments I can feel my breathing and heart rate slowing down—and I can practically feel my blood pressure dropping!—all by themselves, simply by stopping, breathing, and observing.

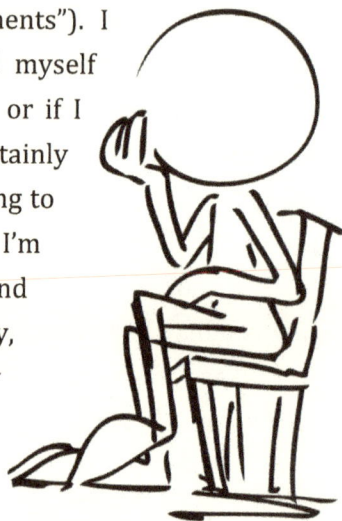

All it takes is a moment to come back to THIS moment!

There are many ways that you can personalize these MMMs. Some people like to put their hands on a table and focus on their palms. Or, if you're not near a desk or table, you can focus on your feet on the floor, feeling the grounding pressure on the soles of your feet. Another option is to carry a "pocket totem" (such as a special coin or a rock) or wear a necklace that serves as a reminder to come back to yourself and back to the present moment.

Regardless of how you experience your MMMs, each one can last for just a few seconds or a few minutes—as long or as short as it takes for you to feel calm, centered, and returned to the present moment—to yourself.

If only I'd been practicing this technique when I got married—I might remember more of my wedding! But at least I have the rest of my life to savor the ongoing present! I hope that MMMs help you to do the same—starting right now. Take a few moments to come back to the present—by focusing on your breath, the soles of your feet, or whatever feels right for you.

Once you're fully present, you'll be able to do what I didn't do: experience and appreciate your own "Big Day"!

Your TMITW Wedding

You have now arrived at the heart of your self-love journey: your "Big Day"—your formal commitment to love, honor, and cherish yourself as long as you live. You will vow to give yourself the unconditional love and support that you would want from an ideal partner—and you will be that partner for yourself!

Think of everything that would be part of your ideal wedding—any rituals or activities that would want to include in your commitment ceremony, all the gifts that you would want to "register" for, and all of the meaningful, symbolic aspects of your wedding.

Show up with your whole self—remembering everything you've discovered about yourself by looking under your "masks," and everything you would look for in another person—a "better half"—and create the most loving, supportive vows that person could ever wish to hear.

Give yourself that sacred gift.

Ceremony

It's extremely powerful to say, "I commit to loving myself unconditionally"—especially if you fully believe the words and feel them resonating throughout your being. It's even more powerful, however, if you reinforce your words, feelings, and commitment with a ceremony.

Just as a wedding ceremony involves rituals that reinforce a couple's love for one another—such as walking down the aisle, saying vows, and exchanging rings—a personal ceremony can help you reinforce your own commitment to loving yourself.

Ceremonies externalize inner experiences—such as maturing, gaining wisdom. They symbolically underscore many of life's most significant passages. They enable us to publicly share a private experience. They make the invisible visible. They link the past, the present, and the future. They connect us with tradition, with society, with something larger than our individual selves.

In your TMITW ceremony, you can create your own rituals—using actions and items that are personally meaningful to you. But

Ceremonies and Rituals

We're so accustomed to ceremonies and rituals that we may not even realize how big a part they play in so many significant moments:

- **Graduation Ceremonies** – including caps and gowns, and special rituals (e.g., moving the tassel when graduation becomes official)

- **Religious Rituals** – such as baptism, confirmation, or bar/bat mitzvah

- **Birthday Parties** – including rituals such as blowing out candles while making a wish

- **Greetings** – such as shaking hands when you meet someone

- **Holidays** – each with their own set of customs (e.g., trick-or-treating on Halloween or eating a big Thanksgiving dinner)

- **Funerals** – and other rituals to honor the dead

...and, of course, **weddings**!

remember that you can also draw from a rich tradition of wedding rituals—some of which you may find powerfully relevant to your individual commitment ceremony (perhaps including some of the traditional elements mentioned below).

Rings

Rings are often exchanged during a wedding ceremony and worn by married couples. While they have different meanings to different people, many see the ring as a symbol the bond between two people and their commitment to love one another. Because a circle never ends, it can be considered a symbol of eternity. Also, in most cultures, the traditional ring finger contains the artery that leads directly to the heart—linking one symbol of love to another!

While you don't have to wear a TMITW ring, you may choose a piece of jewelry, a pocket totem, or some other physical object that you can keep with you most (or all) of the time to serve as a reminder of your loving commitment to yourself.

Officiant

Whether weddings are performed by a religious/spiritual leader or by a justice of the peace, there is generally an officiant who connects the individuals to something larger than themselves—be it the state and the law, or a higher power (couples who see themselves as being married in the eyes of God).

I now pronounce you...YOU!

Is there a person who can symbolically link you with something bigger than your individual life? Would you like someone to perform a ceremony that invests your commitment with an element of the sacred—or even just makes it feel more "official"?

Witnesses

Most weddings are not legally recognized unless there is at least one witness—and usually there are many more!

Aside from the legal aspects (such as signing the marriage license), witnesses help to support you, celebrate you, and multiply your joy. They turn a private experience into a powerful, public declaration. And they see you.

Have you seen the movie *Avatar*? (If not, don't worry—no spoilers ahead!) If so, remember their greeting: "I see you." So simple, yet so powerful! To be seen for who you are. To be witnessed in your most significant moments, your most vulnerable moments, your most life-affirming moments. Or just to be seen, period. Sometimes this is the greatest gift we can give or receive.

This applies to almost all aspects of life. We want to know that we are seen—that we are not invisible, that our actions are noticed (and, hopefully, appreciated), that our voices are heard, that we are known for who we truly are.

While a private individual ceremony can be very powerful, I hope you'll consider including at least one witness in your TMITW wedding—a person to champion you, celebrate your commitment, and share your joy.

Help

As we noted in the previous chapter, a LOT goes into planning and carrying out a wedding! It is very rare for a single person to do it all themselves. There's generally a whole team of helpers who take care of a wedding's many details—from fixing the bride's make-up to cooking and serving the food. Families, bridesmaids, best men, caterers, hair dressers, and many other helpers generally get recruited to make sure that the wedding day is as special as possible.

Even if your TMITW ceremony isn't as elaborate as a fancy wedding, you still might want to ask for help—even if it's just having a friend pick up some take-out food for the occasion. The key is to remember that *you deserve help*—and loving friends or family members are generally glad to lend a hand.

Personalize It!

Although there are numerous traditional elements to draw from, the key is to personalize your ceremony (and your life) so that it reflects you, your style, and your deepest values.

Regardless of how big or small you make it, I hope you'll consider performing your own personal TMITW "wedding" ritual. You can make it similar to a traditional wedding, or you can make it completely different—whatever form is most meaningful to *you*.

After all, this is *your* big day!

> *Personalize your ceremony (and your life) so that it reflects you, your style, and your deepest values.*

Reception

Your TMITW ceremony is one of the most important steps in your journey of self-love! You've given yourself such a beautiful, loving gift—now all that's left to do is to fully receive it...with a full reception!

A reception can mean different things to different people. In traditional weddings, it often includes music, dancing, cake, and friends or family making embarrassing speeches. It's also generally a time when the newlyweds receive presents, which is appropriate, since, at its heart, the word reception means to *receive*. And this is a huge step in your self-love process: the ability to graciously receive.

Just as it is so important to "register" or ask for what we would like, it is also critical to be able to receive what is given— whether it is a beautiful "present" moment or a literal present, such as a wedding gift.

When you do get a gift—for a wedding or any other occasion (or "just because")—there are several approaches you could take:

- **You could refuse to accept it** – simply saying, "No, I didn't ask for this! I don't want it! I won't take it!"

- **You could accept it after much hemming and hawing** – for instance, saying, "Oh, no, I couldn't possibly accept this—it's far too extravagant! You shouldn't have!"

- **Or you could simply accept it** – and just say, "Thank you." Period.

Which approach do you think would make the giver feel better? Which approach do you think would make *you* feel better?

Of course: just saying thank you!

Imagine if you gave someone a wedding present (or a Christmas present, birthday present, just-because present, or simply a favor) and they refused to accept it. How would that make you feel? You went out of your way to pick something out that you thought they'd like, you paid good money for it, and took the time and effort to give it to them—only to have your gift rejected.

What an insult!

The same is true, to some extent, if someone protests or is reluctant to accept your gift for some reason. It makes the giver feel unappreciated.

The best gift that you can give a gift-giver is to graciously accept a gift—to say thank you and show your appreciation.

This doesn't mean that you necessarily have to love the gift— or even keep it. It simply means that you acknowledge the giver—including the time, effort, thought and/or money that they put into the gift.

Non-wedding Gifts

This applies to gifts of all kinds—including favors or compliments. If someone offers to do something nice for you, let them! If someone pays you a compliment, don't reject it. How often have you heard—or been part of—an exchange along the lines of:

Person #1: You look great!
Person #2: Oh, no—I'm a mess, my clothes are wrinkled, and I've got bags under my eyes!

You can probably guess how Person #1 feels—pretty crummy, right? They might even think twice before paying another compliment to Person #2 (or anyone else, for that matter). Regardless of how Person #2 felt, what would have been the harm of simply saying, "Thank you"?

If you really do feel bad about your appearance (or whatever someone compliments you about), you can honestly add, "That means a lot to me—especially now, when I'd been feeling down on myself. You really boosted my self-esteem"...or whatever words feel natural to you.

Receiving at Work

This principle holds true in many situations—not just regarding gifts. Learning to *accept* keeps energy flowing, whereas rejecting (gifts, compliments, or ideas) shuts it down. Learning to receive graciously can help you in a marriage, in other close personal relationships, and just about anywhere else—even at work.

For instance, say that you manage a company and an employee comes to you with an idea. Let's imagine two very different scenarios...

Scenario #1:

Employee: Hey, boss—I've got a great idea! What if instead of requiring everyone to be here Monday-Friday, 9-5, we let people set their own hours—as long as they work 40 hours per week?

Manager: That's a stupid idea! Don't you know that we all have to be here at the same time? What's wrong with you?!

(Even if you're not a manager or employee, you might recognize this sort of internal "conversation" between the subpersonalities within your own head—complete with an overly harsh "critic"!)

Whether this is a real-life scenario or simply an internal dialogue, how do you think the employee would feel after getting this reaction? Pretty deflated and embarrassed, I'd imagine. They'd also probably be very reluctant to open up to the manager ever again about *any* ideas.

Compare this with **Scenario #2:**

Manager: Interesting idea. I'll definitely think that over. Please always feel free to share any other ideas you get!

(In terms of subpersonalities, the scenario-two manager might represent your inner cheerleader or champion—a great voice to have on your side!)

In a real-life work environment, whether or not the manager actually implements the idea, think of the difference in how the employee would feel. I imagine they would feel validated, valued, heard, appreciated, or at least acknowledged. In *Avatar* terms, they would be SEEN! Even if the manager didn't adopt that exact suggestion, at least their relationship with the employee would probably be infinitely better with this dynamic as opposed to instantly shooting them down.

Aside from helping interpersonal relationships, you can almost always benefit from input. On a practical level, even if a specific idea didn't make sense for some reason, just considering it might lead to another idea that would work. (In the example used above, maybe employees could choose from three schedule options, allowing them to work earlier or later depending on their preference.) Or, even if the idea didn't lead to anything, the employee in Scenario #2 would probably be more open to sharing ideas in the future, some of which might be fantastic!

If this dynamic holds true for adults, just think of how much more powerfully it applies to impressionable children. When they are curious and excited about sharing their ideas, think of the difference between being encouraged as opposed to immediately being shot down (or shut down), told why they're wrong, why their ideas are stupid or, worse yet, why *they* are stupid.

If children, employees, and spouses can benefit simply from being seen, heard, and encouraged—in other words, by having people graciously receive whatever they offer (gifts, ideas, or compliments)—don't you think you could also benefit the same way? Don't you think you deserve to have your gifts received with grace—and, in turn, to graciously receive others' gifts?

You Deserve It!

A huge part of your self-love journey is feeling that you deserve to receive: compliments, help, and gifts of all kinds. But it doesn't always come naturally to some people (especially if they've grown up with models who found it difficult to receive). I get this. For most of my early life, whenever I was paid a compliment I became awkward and uncomfortable, as if the world had gotten smaller. I never felt like I was good enough or deserved compliments, gifts, or even love.

If you've ever felt this way, I understand this awkwardness, but I implore you to look deep down inside and recognize the power of gracious receiving. It has taken me years to master the simple response of saying "thank you"—and meaning it!—but I now realize that expressing appreciation to someone who gives you a gift or a compliment is the best gift you can give back to them...and to yourself!

Time to Tie the Knot!

So, now it's time to give and receive one of the most precious gifts imaginable: self-love. You're ready to commit to being your own better half, to celebrate your love, and to savor each precious moment of the ceremony and the reception—and the rest of your life!

~ EXERCISES ~

Coming Back to Now, Coming Back to You

MMMs – Many Meditative Moments

Try a "Meditative Moment" right now (as soon as you finish reading these sentences). Take three deep breaths, and then simply breathe naturally. See if you can notice your breathing slowing down. Can you feel and/or hear your heartbeat? Is it slowing down, too? Consciously pull in your energy, collecting yourself, focusing on this present moment—for as much (or as little) time as feels right for you.

Simply BE...

When you've given yourself enough time to come back to yourself and this moment, describe your experience. How did it feel while you were doing it? In what way(s) do you feel different now than you did before your meditative moment? _____

_____

_____

_____

_____

MMM with Movement:

You can also add the following movement: While taking the deep breaths, put your arms over your head during the inhalation. On the exhalation, bend over forward and stretch your arms in front of you to relax your neck and shoulders. Repeat this as many times as feels right to you. After trying this exercise, do you feel more relaxed? More focused? Any other experiences or sensations?

_____

_____

_____

_____

_____

Personalized MMMs

What are some other types of personalized MMMs that you could try (e.g., focusing on the soles of your feet against the floor)? Be creative! Consider some possibilities that feel like YOU! _____

_____

_____

_____

_____

Reminders

*What are some physical reminders to come back to the present? Do you have a special object that could serve as an MMM trigger (e.g., a religious necklace, a favorite rock or gemstone, or some other "pocket totem" that you could keep with you most—or all— of the time)?*_____

_____

_____

_____

_____

*What are some situational reminders to come back to the present (e.g., when you're stopped at a red light or waiting in a line)? It can be any situation that you find yourself in from time to time— especially those that might normally trigger frustration or other negative responses.*_____

_____

_____

_____

_____

Writing, Reading, and Reflecting on Your Vows

Write "wedding" vows for yourself!

What do you vow to yourself? Do you promise to always do your best for yourself, to take care of yourself, to love yourself unconditionally? Do you vow to treat yourself as well as you would treat a beloved partner? Do you vow to honor your physical body and nurture your mind and spirit?

These are YOUR personal vows—so make them speak to you. Whether you share them with a roomful of your "champions" or just a single loved one, make these vows resonate with your own heart. They are for you—in your own words and your own style.

Make them as formal and traditional, or as casual and creative as you'd like—just make them represent you and the love that you promise to give yourself from this day forward, unconditionally, as long as you live. _____

_____

_____

_____

_____

_____

_____

_____

_____

_____

_____

_____

_____

_____

_____

_____

_____

_____

_____

_____

(Use as much additional paper as necessary.)

Read Your Vows

After you've finished writing your vows, read them aloud to yourself. Experience each word resonating within you. Feel the love that you are expressing—from yourself, for yourself.

Reflect on Your Vows

*How did you feel while writing and reading your vows? What thoughts or emotions arose within you? How do you feel different than you did before you wrote and read these vows?*_____

_____

_____

_____

_____

_____

How do you think your life will be different now that you've taken these vows? _____

_____

_____

_____

_____

_____

Your TMITW Wedding Ceremony

Take as much (or as little) time as you'd like to plan, prepare, and perform a ceremony that represents your commitment to yourself. It can be simple or elaborate, long or short, public or private— anything that has personal significance.

Planning

What will you do for your commitment ritual—your personal "To Me I Thee Wed" wedding ceremony? How does it represent you— your values, your style, and your commitment to loving yourself?

_____

_____

_____

_____

_____

_____

Preparation

*What do you need to do to prepare for your ceremony (e.g., a ring, flowers, decorations)?*_____

_____

_____

_____

_____

_____

Ceremony

After you have performed your ceremony, describe it here. What did you do? How did it feel? What does it mean to you? And how will it affect your life from this point forward?

_____

_____

_____

_____

_____

_____

~~~~~~

Being a gracious receiver

Write about a time when you've been offered a gift of any kind (including physical presents, compliments, or even ideas/suggestions). Did you hem and haw (e.g., "No, I couldn't possibly..."), did you accept the gift graciously, or did you reject it? How did you feel? How do you think the giver felt? Were you uncomfortable when you received the gift? Why? _____

_____

_____

_____

_____

Same question as above, but this time, write about a time when YOU were the one giving (or offering) a gift. _____

_____

_____

_____

_____

Ongoing Exercise: Gracious Receiving

In the future, when you're giving, receiving, or even observing others giving/receiving, notice whether or not the gift is received graciously. How does the accepting (or rejecting) affect the energy of the situation? How does it impact the relationship of the people involved? How does your ability to accept graciously reflect your capacity for self-love?

The Magic Continues...

So, now you've fully committed to loving, honoring, and cherishing yourself for as long as you live. Does that mean your journey is over?

Far from it! In fact, it's just beginning—you still have the rest of your life to honor this commitment. You still have a lifetime of love and magic to look forward to—starting with one of the most magic times of all: *your own personal wedding night and honeymoon!*

Chapter Six

The Wedding Night

and

The Honeymoon

~ Whisking Yourself Away ~

My husband wanted me to have the perfect honeymoon. And, like our engagement, he wanted it to be a surprise—so much so that he told me to pack two suitcases: one for hot weather, one for cold. So as I headed off on my first voyage as a married woman, I didn't have a clue about where I was going (which, in retrospect, seems fitting!).

He drove us to a train station in Indianapolis. Now, to you, this might not seem like a thrilling start to a honeymoon. To me, however, it was the height of romance.

You see, Rick and I had talked about all the things I had never done in my life that I wanted to do: for instance, I had never watched the movies *Gone with the Wind* or *Alice in Wonderland*, I had never played Scrabble, and I had never ridden on a train.

So as I boarded the train, I realized that, first of all, Rick had been paying attention, and also that he was determined that I would indeed experience all the things I had dreamed about.

I can't say, however, that the trip lived up to Rick's idea of a fantasy honeymoon. I'm sure he had many dreams of how our romantic train ride would go—including many amorous episodes in our cozy little sleeper car. Due to my past baggage and issues associated with intimacy, however, let's just say that his new bride was less than pliant.

Nonetheless, Rick showed the utmost patience with me, and we both enjoyed the trip. I still had no idea where we were heading, but I loved taking in the breathtaking scenery as we headed from Indianapolis all the way out west through the mountains.

Aside from the intimacy issue, the only other problem was that the train was so shaky that it made it difficult to sleep or even walk. But even this seemed fitting: a shaky start to our marriage, but all part of the experience, the adventure, and the fear/discomfort/excitement of pushing past my comfort zone and trying something new.

The Wedding Night

Traditionally, the wedding night was (supposedly) the first sexual experience. Although this is increasingly rare in modern times, some couples still wait until marriage. But regardless of whether or not the wedding night is a person's "first time," it is still an occasion loaded with significance: a union of bodies and hearts, the consummation of a marriage. It's a night full of intimacy, fantasy, and sensuality—and other elements that can apply just as much to you as an individual!

Sensuality

Although it's commonly associated with sex, the word "sensuality" actually relates to your five senses: what you see, hear, touch, taste, and smell.

Sometimes we can focus so much on thoughts and emotions—the mind, heart, and spirit—that we neglect our bodies. This includes proper nutrition, rest, and exercise—but it's so much more than that. Your body is not some unfeeling machine that you merely need to keep in good working order. To be a full, vibrant, human, you need to experience sensual pleasure and joy!

This might mean getting a massage—not just because you have a sore back, but because it feels good. It might mean eating a wonderful meal—not just because it's healthy, but because it's delicious and you enjoy savoring every bite (being a gourmet rather than a gourmand or a glutton). And yes, it might mean enjoying healthy, pleasurable sex—not merely for procreation.

If you live most of your life in your head—or even in your heart or spirit—then maybe it's time to "come to your senses" and add some sensuality to your life!

Intimacy

Sensuality and physical pleasure can be a huge, wonderful part of the wedding night—or any sexual encounter. What makes sex transcend mere physical pleasure, however, is intimacy.

Intimacy is private—it is something that you share with a special person, not with the entire world. It implies emotional closeness, understanding, connection, a sense of vulnerability. It involves contact—eye contact, skin-to-skin contact, heart-to-heart contact. It means slowing down long enough to really see someone, experiencing a moment without speeding past or rushing over it.

Intimacy also implies depth. When you have an intimate knowledge of a subject, it means that you have a deep understanding of it. Likewise, when you are truly intimate with someone, it means that you go beyond superficialities. You experience the depth of the person and the relationship.

On the other hand, you can "know" someone for years—spending time together, interacting, and learning about many details of their life—without ever developing any intimacy.

The same thing holds true for you as an individual: You spend every waking moment of your entire life with yourself, yet how often do you experience true intimacy? How often do you connect with yourself at a deep level?

Do you tend to rush through your days, or do you take time to slow down, see the details, and savor the moment? Do you spend most of your time with others, or do you frequently have privacy? Do you give yourself time, space, and *permission* to spend intimate time with yourself, to sink beneath the surface, to truly connect with yourself?

Self-Exploration, Self-Expansion, and Self-Revelation

One of the most exciting parts of intimacy is *revelation*: discovering new aspects of people and things you thought you knew—including yourself!

When you unveil yourself—removing layer after layer of "masks" or clothing or anything else that covers up your true, inner self—you become more exposed. This can leave you feeling vulnerable or uncomfortable.

Where did you go, Self? You must be around here somewhere!

You may find that you judge yourself. You may not always like what you see under the veils—whether it's a birthmark, a scar, or a belief that contradicts the picture you hold of yourself (your "representative"). You may expose a shadow side that rarely sees the light of day. You might feel very uncomfortable and wish to scurry back to cover—back to the safety of the familiar.

But the shadow side is nothing you need to be afraid of. After all, we all contain different sides within ourselves—yin and yang, optimism and pessimism, and the whole range of human qualities. These complexities—even apparent contradictions—make us fuller, richer human beings rather than two-dimensional caricatures.

Remember, exposing and exploring your shadow side—or any part of you that usually remains covered up—doesn't mean that it will consume you. You don't have to rearrange your entire life just because you recognize something different in yourself. It just means that you are expanding yourself—and becoming more understanding of others.

For instance, if you realize that you can see the wisdom of a political position you normally oppose, that doesn't mean you have to rush out and change your political party. You might not even agree with it completely, but perhaps you'll understand how others might—and maybe think twice before condemning them with unkind labels.

Our shadows can make us more compassionate toward others. (Perhaps we'll judge others less harshly if we acknowledge an aspect of ourselves in their beliefs, actions, or anything else we find objectionable about them.) Our shadows can help us see the shades of gray in the world, in others, and in ourselves—and remind us that there is far more to us than the sliver we generally acknowledge.

> ### Revealing your true self
> —shadow side, uncertainties, vulnerabilities, shades of gray, "warts and all"—can be one of the greatest acts of love you can give to anyone... especially yourself!

As we become more intimate with ourselves, we shine a light on our shadows and illuminate our true depths—parts of which might be pleasantly surprising, and other parts of which might be unsettling or unpleasant. I certainly don't want to give the impression, however, that revealing yourself is necessarily a difficult, uncomfortable process. Just like on your wedding night or honeymoon, stripping down (in any sense) can be very exciting, stimulating, and downright sexy! Revealing your true self—shadow side, uncertainties, vulnerabilities, shades of gray, "warts and all"—can be one of the greatest acts of love you can give to anyone...*especially* yourself! It can turn your fantasies into realities!

The Other Side of Fantasy

Throughout this book we've considered the difference between reality and fantasy—especially romantic fantasies. Sometimes fantasies can lead to unhealthy, unrealistic expectations; yet fantasies aren't inherently bad. They're natural and universal. Every person, family, and culture harbors fantasies.

When you were younger, you may have had fantasies of a knight in shining armor (or some modern equivalent, such as a big house, fancy car, and highly successful tech company) sweeping you off your feet. You may have had fantasies of finding your soul mate and living happily ever after—without a problem or a care in the world. You may have had fantasies about someone coming into your life and fixing everything that you don't like about your life and yourself.

Unfortunately, as appealing as these fantasies seem, they usually end the same way: disappointment. The knight turns out to be a fool. The prince turns out to be a frog. Or, even if Mr. Right is every bit as wonderful as you'd hoped, that doesn't mean that he can "fix" you. (And if he tries, that can be even more annoying than if he doesn't!) Or maybe the reality isn't bad at all—just different from what you'd hoped and imagined.

Fantasies can be wonderful dreams, but eventually we wake up to reality—with all of its messiness, gray areas, and contradictions. This doesn't mean, however, that fantasies can't be very positive and helpful. Fantasies are another form of dreams, visions of our ideal lives, and embodiments of our highest values and goals. They can serve as beacons from within—like inner "vision boards" leading us toward our greatest hopes and fullest potential.

Also, not all fantasies turn out to be false. We may have a fantasy about a romantic wedding night, and then have the actual night live up to our hopes in every way—or even surpass them. We may have a fantasy or vision of ourselves inspiring other people with our words—only to make this fantasy into a reality beyond our wildest dreams! We may have a fantasy of ourselves surrounded by a happy, loving family—and create a family that's even more loving than what we imagined.

Although I've spent a lot of time cautioning and urging you not to get caught up in unrealistic fantasies (or delusions), I certainly don't want to dissuade you from harboring dreams, hopes, and visions of a wonderful life. These visions can motivate you to achieve greatness, they can keep you going through rough times, and they can guide you toward a brighter future.

Sometimes we realize or even surpass our fantasies. But even if we don't, just having those fantasies can get us moving in a positive direction. We might end up at a very different destination than we'd planned—perhaps even more appealing than our fantasy. But we might not have had the courage, motivation, or initiative to even get moving at all if we didn't have a fantasy spurring us on.

> *Dreams, hopes, and visions of a wonderful life can motivate you to achieve greatness, keep you going through rough times, and guide you toward a brighter future.*

My Honeymoon (Part II): Fantasy and Fear

When our honeymoon train finally reached its destination, I realized that I definitely wouldn't be needing those tropical clothes I'd packed. We were going skiing in Montana!

This truly was a fantasy come true! We were staying at a fabulous resort, surrounded by towering mountains and snowcapped skylines. The scenery was breathtaking, and the skiing promised to be exhilarating.

While I was enthralled by this step beyond my known comfort zone, it also filled me with a rush of fear. Spending most of my life in the small town of Versailles, Ohio, I found this all a bit overwhelming. I had been skiing before—at a small slope with one hill with one ski lift—but to be on a mountain with multiple ski lifts and such grandeur left me in a state of awe...*and panic!* I was afraid of the ski lift. I was afraid of the snow. I was afraid of falling. I was afraid of looking like a fool in front of my new husband. I was just afraid, period!

Fortunately, Rick knew better than to try to get me out on the slopes right away. Instead, he first took me to a place that he thought would help ease my nervousness. So it was that at 10 a.m. on the first morning of our honeymoon, I found myself perched on a red-leather barstool.

When my husband asked the bartender what would be a good shot for me, he replied, "the snake bite." Oh my, what an apropos name! The drink tasted sweet and strong, and it gave me the shot of courage I so badly needed—or at least enough to get me out of the tavern and onto the slopes!

But my newfound courage quickly drained when I found myself high up on the world's biggest ski lift (or at least that's how it seemed to me in that moment). Throughout the vertiginous climb, my legs dangled precariously under my narrow perch, and my heart raced with trepidation. Rather than enjoying the scenery above and around me, I fixated on the vast space between my skis and the ground far below. All the "what-if's" came flooding in, leading me up a path of escalating fear and panic.

My husband must have sensed my anxiety, because he took my hand and reassured me, letting me know that this fear could be in my control and that I needed to allow myself the pleasure of the experience. I can't say that I entirely released my fear, but I did manage to become more present—and even pry my gaze away from the expanse of empty space directly beneath me!

The view was amazing, especially from this bird's-eye perspective. The snow-covered pine trees looked like something from another world—dark-green aliens, bent under the weight of the snowy cover, their spiny limbs protruding at odd angles, as if they were emerging from enormous, white cocoons.

Despite my fear and discomfort, I decided that it was time for me to emerge as well—to leave the warm safety of my familiar world, stretch my limbs, and explore this strange, menacing, and magnificent terrain in which I found myself.

I decided it was time to live in the present moment and allow myself to feel exhilarated despite the fear and discomfort. It was time to put on my explorer's hat and leave the safety of my cocoon. It was time to leap out of my comfort zone and into a new world of confidence and exploration.

It was time for me to grow.

YOUR Honeymoon

After the wedding night, one of the most common fantasies people have—and experience—is the honeymoon. Many people dream about, plan, and actually live an extended fantasy immediately after their weddings.

Aside from the romance and (for some) intimacy, the honeymoon is a time for newlyweds to unwind after the excitement (and, frequently, stress) of a wedding. It's a time to spend quality time together—away from family, friends, and the multitudes that are normally part of wedding (the guests, as well as planners, caterers, and all the others who help with the planning and the event itself). *It's a time to reflect, to celebrate, to relax, to exhale, to look back and to look forward to your life together—but also, perhaps more than anything else, to simply enjoy the present moment.*

But you don't have to get married to enjoy these benefits. Taking time to reflect, relax, and recharge any time you need to can restore your sense of balance and well-being. Taking time to renew your body and soul away from your

Where does the word "honeymoon" come from?

Honeymoons have been around for centuries, although they've meant very different things to different people over the years. Theories abound regarding the origin of the word itself:

Some claim that the word originates from Ancient Babylon, where it was customary to drink mead (a honey-based alcohol) for a lunar month after a wedding.

Another explanation is that it refers to the tendency of love to wane—like the moon.

Perhaps the most surprising explanation is that it's from the Norse word for kidnapping, hjunottsmanathr, as it was common Nordic practice (in ancient times!) to kidnap one's bride-to-be and keep her hidden away until she either became pregnant or her family stopped looking for her!

["honeymoon." *Online Etymology Dictionary.* Retrieved 2010-08-03] busy life can restore your passion for that life—even when you return to it.

You can give yourself a personal "honeymoon" any time you feel the need for some self-care, but you might especially appreciate it after a big event or achievement. Whether it's a wedding, finishing a creative project, or getting a promotion at work, give yourself time to relax and savor the moment before diving headlong into the next project.

Buffers, Rewards, and Downtime

Aside from the pleasure of a honeymoon—newlyweds basking in the glow of one another's love, often in exotic locations—another great aspect is that it provides a buffer between your wedding and your everyday life. Can you imagine having a lavish wedding, followed by a romantic wedding night, followed by...getting up and going to work (and going grocery shopping, running errands, and performing household chores) *just like any other day?*

How depressing!

Not that there's necessarily anything wrong with your everyday life—it can be wonderful! But wouldn't it also be wonderful to savor this special time for a while rather than race right past it?

Yet how many times in your own life do you experience a momentous occasion, only to resume "business as usual" almost immediately? How often do you strive to reach some goal, promising yourself a reward once the striving is over—only to reach the goal but not reward yourself. Perhaps you simply forget, or you're too busy, or you don't think the reward itself is important.

This is what happened to me and Rick. We always said that we'd go to Tahiti once we paid off our student loans. Well, after years of hard work, frugal living, and diligent payments, we finally paid off the last of the loans—over $200,000 worth! But we put off our trip to Tahiti. We were too busy. Life kept getting in the way. It just wasn't the right time.

And, as so often happens, it was never "the right time"—so we never took that trip, never celebrated this momentous achievement. We let the moment pass, continuing along with our everyday lives—and I still regret it to this day. Even though the loans are paid off, I still feel a sense of incompleteness—like a sentence without a period at the end. (Maybe writing and reflecting on this will be just the impetus I need to prove that it's never too late to celebrate!)

Regardless of what goals you set for yourself or what rewards you have planned for when you reach them, I urge you not to neglect to celebrate your achievements—*before* the moment passes.

But even if you never give yourself the planned reward, it still serves its purpose, right? It motivates you to reach your goal—and that's what's *really* important, right?

Well, yes. But the reward is important, too! Celebrating a milestone is a vital part of any process. Taking time to savor momentous occasions can be as valuable as the occasions themselves! Celebrations acknowledge the value of the occasion. Also (although you never need to justify rewarding yourself for a job well done) rewards help motivate you to reach future goals—and create even more momentous occasions to celebrate!

Aside from this, after a big push and a big event, your body (and mind and spirit) just need some downtime—for your own health and sanity! It's only natural. Fields yield more crops if they're allowed to lie fallow after producing a harvest. Many animals hibernate during the winter—and all animals sleep. Even God took a day off after a busy week! Don't you deserve a break as well?

The Honeymoon Trip

In addition to providing a break and a buffer between the wedding and the resumption of everyday life, a honeymoon also provides an opportunity to travel—which has two huge benefits: 1. the experience of being somewhere else, and 2. the fact that it can change the way you experience your at-home life when you return. In this sense, you can enjoy your trip for the rest of your life!

It's a common belief that "travel broadens the mind," but not all travel involves hopping on a boat or a plane. Voyages come in many forms and varieties: They can be literal trips to faraway destinations. They can be new experiences right in your own home town. They can be short getaways from your normal surroundings and normal routine. They can be anything that refreshes and recharges you or changes your perspective.

As Margaret Mead said, "It is not the act of traveling that broadens our minds, but the mindset that travels along with us that will bring a person far in life." And that broadening starts with having an open mind—being receptive to new experiences, to differences, to novelty.

The Importance of Novelty

To put a twist on the old saying: Familiarity doesn't breed contempt—it breeds invisibility! We can cease to notice things that are overly familiar. We become accustomed to our routine. We can even take people for granted.

On the other hand, when we experience something new and different, we have no choice but to pay attention. The human brain thrives on novelty. New places, people, and experiences cause our minds to wake up and our senses to spring to life.

And this phenomenon frequently carries over after a trip is completed. It's common for people returning from overseas to experience "reverse culture-shock"—seeing their once-familiar lives through new eyes. Sometimes this can inspire people to make a shift in the way they're living, or it can simply help them gain greater appreciation for their lives exactly as they are!

In either case, sometimes a trip (or any other novel experience) is just what we need to shake us up, wake us up, and help us see the world in a new light.

Whether you're married or single, you can experience many of the benefits of your own personal honeymoon voyage— enjoying every step of the way: from planning and packing to the actual vacation and the trip back home—seeing your life with a fresh set of eyes...and maybe even a broadened mind!

> *The human brain thrives on novelty.*
> *New places, people, and experiences*
> *cause our minds to wake up and*
> *our senses to spring to life.*

Dreaming and Planning

Before you plan a honeymoon (or any other experience), feel free to dream! Let your imagination run wild! Consider all the possibilities—and even the impossibilities! Think about all of the things that bring you to life, that wake you up and make your heart jump for joy! What sort of trip or experience would celebrate who you are—while offering the possibility of expanding who you are?

If you were going on a honeymoon-style trip, where would you go? What would you do? What would you bring? Would you want to go somewhere relaxing or invigorating? Would you want to try something completely new and foreign to you, or would you prefer the comfort of a familiar place/experience?

Imagine that you had an unlimited amount of time and money—and that you could choose any destination and activities (or lack thereof) that appealed to you. Where would you go, and what would you do?

"Do Not Disturb"

One additional benefit of a honeymoon—whether taken alone or with a partner—is the chance to use three of the sexiest words in the English language: *Do Not Disturb!*

These words—especially when printed on a sign and hung on a hotel door handle—conjure images of romance, sensuality, passion, and perhaps even a hint of mystery, intrigue, and excitement. It is a sign (often literally) that you are shutting out the world, spending time with someone you know intimately—and, most likely, want to know even more intimately. Perhaps this person is your spouse, perhaps a new friend—or perhaps yourself!

Despite the sexy connotations, these three words are among the most important words possible when it comes to spending quality time with yourself. Although it's widely accepted for couples to put up a "Do Not Disturb" sign (literally or figuratively), it's far less common for individuals to request undisturbed time alone. Yet shutting out the world from time to time is one of the greatest gifts you can give yourself. It helps you get to know yourself better. It helps you accomplish goals. It helps you work more productively. And it sends a clear signal to the outside world that you value yourself, you set clear boundaries, you make self-care a priority, and, most of all, that *you're worth it!*

Whether you're going on a personal honeymoon, working on a creative project, or simply looking for some undisturbed time to recharge and regroup after spending a lot of time in public, you might benefit from some "Do Not Disturb" time of your own! This could mean going away on a private retreat, unplugging the phone, or simply unplugging from the internet for a day—and plugging back into your own life!

Mini-Moons

Even if you don't have the time or the budget for a full-blown, honeymoon-style vacation right now, you can always benefit from "mini-moons"—small trips, new experiences, or any changes in your routine or surroundings that help you get a new perspective. This could mean taking a day trip, meeting new people, reading a book or seeing a movie in a very different genre from your normal tastes, going to the park for a moment of mind clearing, or simply taking a different route home from work—and exploring a different part of town.

Ultimately, the importance of travel isn't that you have to do something on a grand scale—just that you open yourself up to new experiences.

New Eyes

In the classic mythological journey, the hero travels to a special world and retrieves a talisman, which he or she then brings back to their "ordinary" world—frequently to the benefit of those who live there. While the mythological talisman may be a sword, a ring, or some other magical object, you might find a real-life talisman during your own personal honeymoon journey. It might be a souvenir, a seashell, a snapshot, or some other object that reminds you of your experience. It might be a friend you made who you stay in touch with even after your trip is done. Or it might be an idea or an insight that helps you with your everyday life—a new way of looking at the world...and yourself!

As Marcel Proust said, "The real voyage of discovery consists not in seeking new landscapes but in having new eyes." When you take a honeymoon—or any other journey—you change your perspective. You change the way you see the world. You change yourself!

See the world through a new lens!

When you take your personal honeymoon (or "mini-moon"), stay open to shifts in perspective. You might see your life in a different light—as if seeing through new eyes! Maybe you'll feel super relaxed—and realize that you'd like to take more time to relax in your everyday life. Maybe you'll visit a place where people are less privileged, and you'll gain a greater appreciation for all you have—or you might choose to get involved in humanitarian projects that help alleviate other people's suffering. Or maybe you'll be introduced to fascinating cultures that help you realize that there are so many different ways of living, so many options and possibilities for your own life!

When you travel around the world or just around the block, it's not the world that changes—it's the way you *see* the world that changes.

Bon Voyage!

You can begin your own voyage of self-exploration and self-celebration right now. Let the exercises below serve as a map, a travel guide, and a ticket to a more joyful YOU!

~ EXERCISES ~

Come to Your Senses!

What are some of your favorite experiences that excite each of your five senses?

*Sight:*_____

_____

_____

_____

Sound: _____

_____

_____

_____

Touch: _____

_____

_____

_____

Taste: _____

_____

_____

Smell: _____

_____

_____

_____

Your TMITW Wedding Night

Plan a sensual "wedding-night" celebration where you incorporate at least one of your favorite experiences from each sense. What will you do for each of your five senses—and for your whole self?

_____

_____

_____

_____

_____

_____

_____

_____

_____

_____

After you've had the "wedding night," describe the experience:

_____

_____

_____

_____

_____

_____

_____

_____

_____

_____

_____

_____

_____

_____

~~~~~~

Individual Intimacy

Becoming Intimate with Your Surroundings

Set aside at least 20 minutes of private time when you know you'll be uninterrupted. Become aware of the elements around you— through your five senses. What do you see, hear, taste, smell, and touch? As you sit silently, do you notice ambient sounds that you're not usually aware of? Do you hear birds? Cars? The hum of a refrigerator? Look around—do you see anything that you don't normally pay attention to? Pick one object and examine it closely. Focus on it for a while. Do you begin to notice any details that you didn't notice at first? If possible, touch it. Feel its weight, its texture, the way it feels in your hands. Does it have a smell? Does it make a sound—either by itself or when you tap it? (Note: Unless it's edible, you probably don't *want to try tasting it!) Spend at least 10 minutes becoming intimate with this object, and then write what you noticed or learned about it (and about yourself) during the experience.* _____

_____

_____

_____

_____

_____

_____

_____

_____

_____

Repeat the above process with *yourself*.

Look at yourself. Focus on details—your freckles, your body hair, your fingernails, or any other detail that you might generally overlook. What do you notice? How has your body changed, matured? _____

_____

_____

_____

_____

_____

_____

Repeat the process one more time, but this time focus on something internal and non-physical (e.g., a thought or emotion).

Really look at it—not with the idea of judging yourself (although if you find judgment arising, you can merely notice that as well), but rather simply seeing *yourself, seeing the truth. Give yourself 10-20 minutes to sit with yourself and just observe. Don't rush! Take your time with yourself. This is your "Me" time! When you're done, write about what you saw, heard, or noticed in any way.*

_____

_____

_____

_____

_____

_____

Shining Light on the Shadow

Suspending Judgment

In order to open up and explore yourself fully, you have to be willing to suspend judgment, even for a little while. (It's very difficult to expose yourself and become vulnerable if you feel criticized at the first sign of something unpleasant!) So, for this exercise, see if you can be as objective as possible while you explore aspects of yourself you might usually suppress.

If you have an unusually strong inner critic, you might appease it by telling it that it will have its turn—that once you are finished with this short process, it will be invited back to speak its piece. But, for now, it's someone else's turn. You might even like to give the inner critic/judge a name. You can also imagine that you're an elementary-school teacher, and the critic is just one of the many students in your class—perhaps a particularly strong-willed and vocal student, who often dominates classroom discussions. But now the other "students" are getting a chance to speak up—especially the very quiet ones who are usually too shy to speak.

Like a good teacher, invite those shy students to participate. And try not to interrupt or cast judgment. Even if they seem stupid or offensive, they might have something of value to add to the classroom discussion. And, if not, you don't have to agree with them—but you can still hear them out.

So, who are some of the "shy students" inside of you? What are their names? What do they have to say? _____

_____

_____

_____

_____

_____

_____

_____

_____

Considering the Other Side

Another way to explore your shadow side is to consider some of your most staunchly defended positions: religious beliefs, political convictions, or any other ideas of what's "right" or what's taboo— and then flip them around: state the opposite position (or even just an entirely different position). But try your best to state this position from the point of view of someone who truly believes it and identifies with it—not as a critic or opponent.

Religious/Spiritual Beliefs

Your belief: _____

_____

_____

_____

Opposite (or very different) belief: _____

_____

_____

_____

Political Beliefs

*Your belief:*_____

_____

_____

_____

*Opposite (or very different) belief:*_____

_____

_____

_____

Moral Beliefs

*Your belief:*_____

_____

_____

_____

*Opposite (or very different) belief:*_____

_____

_____

_____

Other Beliefs (what you consider "right")

*Your belief:*_____

_____

_____

_____

*Opposite (or very different) belief:*_____

_____

_____

_____

Taboo

Something you consider a taboo: _____

_____

_____

_____

Position of someone who believes that this "taboo" is really OK:

_____

_____

_____

Self-Reflection

After completing the exercises above, how do you look at things differently? Are you able to see shades of gray (rather than just black and white)? Have you softened on any positions? Or, even if you haven't changed within yourself, do you feel less judgmental— toward others and toward yourself? _____

_____

_____

_____

_____

_____

_____

_____

_____

_____

_____

_____

_____

_____

~~~~~~

Fantasize This!

Youthful Fantasy

When you were young, what is a fantasy you had—a hope or image of your ideal future? How did it compare to the reality that emerged? _____

_____

_____

_____

_____

_____

Current Fantasy

*What is one fantasy that you still hold today?*_____

_____

_____

_____

_____

_____

_____

Do you truly believe that this fantasy could become a reality? If so, what is one step that you could take today toward that fantasy?

_____

_____

_____

_____

_____

_____

One-Night Fantasy

Fantasies are not always huge life-goals. Just like a couple might have a fantasy wedding night, you could have a fantasy night— with a romantic partner, with friends, or even by yourself. What is a fantasy night that you could realistically experience in the near future (without winning the lottery or somehow landing a dream date with your celebrity crush)? _____

_____

_____

_____

_____

Plan the fantasy night you described above, and DO it (or the closest possible equivalent). Then come back and describe your experience here: _____

_____

_____

_____

_____

_____

_____

Bucket-List Fantasies

Now make your "bucket list"—any fantasies (big, small, serious, silly, or anything else that appeals to you) that you'd like to live out while you're still alive. _____

_____

_____

_____

~~~~~~

Beyond the Comfort Zone

When have you pushed outside of your comfort zone?

This could include traveling, trying a new (and possibly scary) activity, or pushing to do or be more than you had done/been before. How did it feel—before, during, and after the experience?

_____

_____

_____

_____

When have you *not* pushed outside of your comfort zone?

When have you had the opportunity or felt a desire to push beyond or comfort zone...but didn't? Do you regret playing it safe and not taking the chance? If you had the opportunity to do it again, what (if anything) would you do differently? If you have a similar opportunity in the future, what would you do? _____

_____

_____

_____

_____

_____

What's your "snake bite"?

While I certainly don't recommend turning to a shot of alcohol every time you need to be brave, it can be helpful to have positive tools or reminders that give you courage, especially when you're stepping out of your comfort zone. It could be a mantra that focuses you, a song that fires you up, a friend who encourages you, or a pocket totem that grounds you. What's your "snake bite" that gives you courage when you need it? How has it helped you? Or, if you don't have one, who or what might be able to serve this role in the future? When might a "snake bite" come in handy? _____

_____

_____

_____

_____

_____

_____

_____

Buffers, Rewards, and Downtime

How do you like to reward yourself after a big push? _____

_____

_____

_____

_____

What's the last time you accomplished a big goal or went through a major experience? Did you give yourself some downtime before going right back into everyday life (or jumping into your next project)? If so, what was your buffer—and how did it feel? If not, how did you feel about moving right onto something else without a break or reward? _____

_____

_____

_____

_____

_____

When's the next big event and/or goal that you think you'll experience? How would you like to reward yourself afterwards? ___

_____

_____

_____

_____

_____

It doesn't have to be a "BIG event"!

How do you like to reward yourself after medium or small events or accomplishments (e.g., a Friday-night movie to celebrate finishing a week of work, or a soak in the tub at the end of a busy day)? _____

_____

_____

_____

_____

Dreaming and Planning Your "Honeymoon"

Describe your ideal "honeymoon":

Where would you go? Would you go alone or with someone else? How long would your trip be? What would you do (or NOT do)? Don't worry about whether or not your options are feasible or even realistic—you might want to go to Fiji, or you might want to go to Mars! For now, just let your imagination run wild with whatever possibilities (or impossibilities) excite you the most! _____

_____

_____

_____

_____

_____

_____

_____

_____

_____

_____

_____

Now that you've let your imagination run wild, pick your most exciting *realistic* option and actually go there!
Yes, I'm suggesting that you actually take a trip—even if it's an overnight at the local Motel 6. It doesn't have to be the ultimate dream-come-true honeymoon (although it could be)—just as long as it's a trip that excites and nourishes YOU! ***So, where are you going to go, and what are you going to do (or not do)?*** _____

_____

_____

_____

_____

_____

_____

_____

_____

_____

Packing

When you pack for a honeymoon (or any other trip), there are a lot of practical considerations: What's the climate? Will I need formal attire? What does the situation call for (e.g., bug spray and hiking boots, or lipstick and high heels)? But it's also important to remember what means the most to YOU! Do you have a diary or journal that you write in regularly—or when you want to record new experiences? Do you have a favorite book that inspires you? Do you like to listen to certain music to relax you, invigorate you, or comfort you when you're away from home (or when you're at home)? Do you have any totems or other tangible items that help bring you joy, bring you back to life, or bring you back to YOU? (Also, remember to leave a little extra room in your bag. You never know what souvenirs or treasures you'll find on your travels that you'll want to bring home with you! And the same holds true for the rest of your life, too: leaving yourself some extra space/time in your life gives you room for pleasant surprises!)

So, aside from essentials (toothbrush, clean clothes, etc.), what will you pack for your personal honeymoon? How is each item meaningful or significant to you? Why are you bringing it?

_____

_____

_____

_____

_____

_____

_____

_____

_____

After you've dreamed, planned, packed, and actually taken a TMITW "honeymoon," come back and describe your experience:

_____

_____

_____

_____

_____

_____

_____

_____

Do Not Disturb

When are some instances when you would benefit from some individual "Do Not Disturb" time? When would you use it (what times, what days of the week)? How might you benefit?

_____

_____

_____

_____

_____

What can you do to request undisturbed time (e.g., make your own sign, schedule time in your house alone, or even go to a hotel alone—and leave that "sexy" sign on the door handle!)? _____

_____

_____

_____

_____

~~~~~~

"Mini-Moons"

What are some "mini-moons" that you could try? (Brainstorm—try to name at least 4-5 possibilities!) _____

_____

_____

_____

_____

Choose one "mini-moon" from your above list, and do it!
Afterwards, write about your experience. How did you feel before, during, and after your mini-moon? Do you have any new ideas or fresh perspectives on your life? _____

_____

_____

_____

_____

_____

~~~~~~

New Eyes, New Life

After taking your personal honeymoon (or "mini-moon") do you see your everyday life differently? Do you have any new ideas or fresh perspectives? Is there anything and/or anyone who you appreciate more because of your experience? How has the experience changed YOU? _____

_____

_____

_____

_____

You CAN take it with you!
What would you like to bring back from your honeymoon? Is there any experience or insight that you'd like to keep with you when you return to your everyday life? Is there anything you'd like to change about how you live? _____

_____

_____

_____

Your Talisman
Do you have a "talisman"—a physical object that reminds you of this insight, power, and/or commitment to change? If so, what is it? If not, can you find or create one? How does it bring you back to the experience of your journey? How does it make your (so-called) "ordinary" world more extraordinary? _____

_____

_____

_____

Over the Moon

As you complete your TMITW honeymoon and return to your "ordinary world," you're about to begin the most significant portion of your journey: *the rest of your life!*

Chapter Seven

Married Life

~ Being Your Own Better Half...for Your WHOLE Life ~

S o far in this book, we've traced the arc of a romantic relationship from the first meeting through the wedding and honeymoon. It's at this point that most fairytales (and many romantic movies) end; however, there's still a whole lot of life left—in most cases, the majority of your life. With all the focus on the romance of courtship and weddings, it's critical that we not forget the decades of day-to-day living that come *after* the honeymoon!

The question we now face is: After a wedding, honeymoon, or other major milestone or personal achievement—*what's left?*

The answer is almost too obvious: EVERYTHING! Every single day for the rest of your life!

The wedding is just one day—marriage is (hopefully, in most cases) for the rest of your life. It's not just a few carefully scripted hours; it's the moment-by-moment living and relating of the rest

> *Self-love* is an ongoing, moment-by-moment process that incorporates all aspects of life.

of your life. It's how you live, day-in/day-out, that determines the quality of your life—far more than a few peak moments or milestones.

The same idea applies to you as an individual. Loving yourself doesn't just mean going to the spa once a month or throwing yourself a birthday party—and then neglecting your needs the rest of the time. It also doesn't mean taking time to feed your mind and spirit, but neglecting your physical body. Self-love is an ongoing, moment-by-moment process that incorporates all aspects of life:

- Physical
- Mental
- Emotional
- Financial
- Spiritual

...as well as all the related activities of daily life—including children/family, creative projects, cooking, cleaning, and everyday housekeeping.

Self-love isn't about being a do-it-all (or a know-it-all or a have-it-all), it's about maintaining a healthy balance, staying vital, and staying connected to YOU! It's about taking responsibility for your happiness and well-being. So, let's look at how you can do exactly that—in every major area of your life.

Physical Health

As a medical doctor, this is a subject near and dear to my heart. I believe that taking care of your physical health is one of the most important pillars of self-love.

I'm honored to be a part of many people's healing process, but I don't think that a doctor is actually a healer. I believe that a doctor is merely an assistant in each person's healing process. While I can educate, advise, and prescribe, it's up to each individual to take responsibility for their own health.

Taking Responsibility for Your Health

When it comes to your physical health, you have two options: 1. You can blame your genes (or other factors beyond your control) for obesity, high cholesterol, or other health problems, or 2. you can accept where you are now and take responsibility for moving closer to your ideal physical condition.

Which option feels more empowering? Which approach is more likely to lead you to the body you want? Which one is going to enhance your quality of life?

Yes, there *are* many factors that contribute to your physical health (or lack thereof)—including genes and other factors beyond your control. However, you still have the ability to choose how to respond to those factors. (As with all areas of life, "response-ability" is key!) The choice is always yours:

- Are you going to eat healthy foods or junk food?
- Are you going to make exercise and movement a regular part of your life, or blame your desk job for your growing waistline?
- Are you going to take responsibility for your own health, or get mad at your doctor when you don't like what they say during your check-ups?

If you think this last example is silly, you're right—but I actually have numerous patients who get actually mad at me for telling them the truth about their physical condition!

I have one obese patient (who I'll call "Mike") who gets angry at me every time he comes to my office—before I even open my mouth! He always starts our conversations with the words, "You are going to be soooooo mad at me…"

My response to him is always the same: "Why do I have a reason to be mad at you? You haven't hurt me in any way."

He then makes it clear that *he's* the one who's actually mad at *me*! He blames me for not helping him get healthier—while rattling off every excuse known to man as to why he couldn't manage even five minutes of exercise since his last visit.

Mike sees me as the one responsible for his poor health. And he expects me to get angry right back at him, which I refuse to do. After all, if I got angry every time a patient failed to follow through on my recommendations, I'd be a very unhappy person! I can prescribe diet, exercise, or medication, but I don't have any medication that cures a lack of accountability.

The only antidote is personal responsibility.

But why do so many people fail to take responsibility for their health (and/or other areas of their lives)? Wouldn't they want to empower themselves? Wouldn't they want to be happy and healthy? Doesn't *everyone* want to be happy and healthy?

After decades of observing human behavior—within and beyond my medical practice—I've come to a somewhat shocking answer:

No.

I believe that not everyone does want to be healthy. But why not? What are they gaining from staying unhealthy?

Secondary gain

I think it's so important to understand the reasons why we maintain unhealthy attitudes and behaviors. If you can understand *why* you may be avoiding healthier attitudes and behaviors, you've taken the first step toward releasing them and replacing them with more responsible self-care. But why *would* you want to hold on to illness, injury, or anything else that's unhealthy?

It's usually easy to see the *cost* of illness or injury: physical pain, incapacitation, loss of independence, and frequently loss of money. What's not always as readily apparent, however, is the *gain* of illness.

On some level, you have to be getting something out of your condition. Although it's often more subtle, there are always secondary gains from being ill. These might include money (in the form of compensation or benefits), sympathy, a guilt-free reason to stay home from work or school, or even just attention.

I have one patient (who I'll call "Bob")—an 88-year old man who lives alone—who comes in almost every week complaining of nasal congestion. I never find anything wrong with him. (He's also seen several specialists, and none of them has found anything physically wrong with him.) But during his examinations, I always ask Bob about his house, his dog, his neighbor, and anything else in his life. After we chat for a while, I always inform him that I have no new treatment ideas. But he responds cheerfully, "That's OK," and leaves with a smile.

My office may quite possibly be Bob's only social contact, and my examinations might be his only physical contact. So I can't help but wonder: what if there were another way for him to receive attention, physical contact, and social interaction? Would he still be plagued by chronic nasal congestion?

Now this is not to say that most people's illnesses aren't real. As a doctor, I know all too well just how real physical symptoms can be. And that's exactly why I want to help my patients find a way out of their conditions! I also know that this perspective might sound cold or even heartless to some readers, but I offer it in the hopes that it helps people release their pain—*and keep the gain!*

In Bob's case, he might be able to release the nasal problems while keeping the gain of attention and interaction by making regular visits to a senior center or joining a social group of some kind.

Exploring secondary gains of an illness can actually benefit you in many ways—and can lead to empowered action. For instance, someone who misses a lot of work due to illness might consider whether or not they truly love their work. If not, switching to a more appealing career might bring a huge physical and emotional gain.

While nobody *wants* to be sick (at least not consciously), part of taking responsibility for your health and your life is to take an honest look at what you might be gaining through illness—and consider how you might gain something similar (or even better) through robust health!

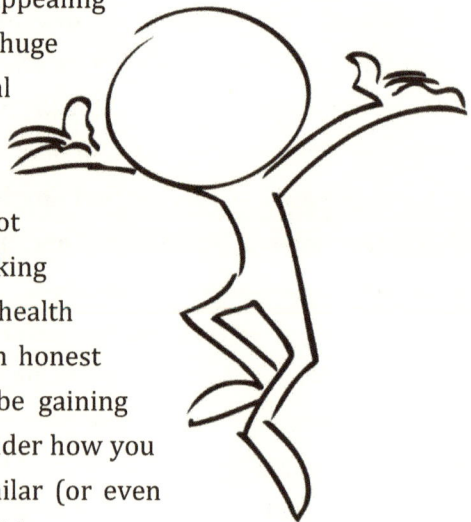

It feels better to feel better!

Mental Outlook and Intellectual Ability

Just as you can choose to take responsibility for your physical health, you're presented with a similar choice regarding your mind. If you're not fully satisfied with your intelligence and/or mental outlook: 1. You can blame your poor education (or blame your younger self for not taking advantage of the opportunities that were available to you), or 2. you can take responsibility for your mental life—starting wherever you are right now and taking steps to move toward reaching your intellectual potential and improving your mental outlook.

Mental Muscles

The phrase "Use it or lose it" definitely applies to your mind!

Just like any other muscle, the mind expands when you use it and atrophies when you don't. So, just like you can strengthen your leg muscles by walking or strengthen your heart through cardiovascular exercise, you can sharpen your mind by keeping it active: reading books, engaging in stimulating conversations, and—perhaps more important than any other factor—exposing yourself to new experiences. The mind thrives on novelty, so "keeping it fresh" is just as important to a brain as it is to a romantic relationship!

Mental Hygiene and Learned Optimism

"Mental hygiene" means much more than being a math whiz, speaking multiple languages, or having a high IQ. It also means having a positive mental outlook. This can aid you in many areas of your life—from physical health, social and business success, and overall happiness and emotional well-being.

One of the most important aspects of this is optimism.

As trite as it may sound, everything that's real—including tangible objects and life experiences—begins with a thought. Thought creates intent, intention creates actions, and action begets results.

This is a powerful chain of events, so it is important to start it off on a good note! The thought is the seed of reality, so if it is a bitter seed, it will yield a bitter reality. On the other hand, optimistic thoughts are much more likely to lead to positive realities.

While some people tend to have a more positive outlook than others, the good news is that even a long-time pessimist can learn to be more optimistic—and reap the rewards of their newfound optimism (which tends to have a positive snowball effect)! And there are many rewards in almost every area of life: optimists tend to be more successful in their careers, experience better physical health, and have happier relationships.

The first step toward a more optimistic outlook is realizing the importance of optimism. Your thoughts, beliefs, and mental outlook tend to be self-fulfilling prophecies, so you have to ask yourself which prophecies you'd like to come true and which beliefs you'd like to prove correct:

- Do you want to prove that all relationships are doomed to fade, or that you can grow closer and more loving with each passing year?
- Do you want to prove that an unexpected challenge is a short-term setback or a permanent failure?
- Do you want to prove that a positive mental outlook can or can't improve your physical health?
- Do you want to believe that you can succeed or that you are destined for failure?

As Henry Ford said, "Whether you think you can, or you think you can't—you're right." So, what (and *how*) do *you* think?

Emotions

Another one of the most important areas of personal responsibility is your emotional life. You might consider emotions to be out of your control—a traffic jam makes you mad, a loved one makes you happy, or a loss makes you sad. Yes, externals do impact our emotions to some degree (especially in the short-term), but probably less than you'd expect. Research estimates that circumstances only account for about 10% of your overall level of happiness!

The truth is that a good deal of your emotional well-being is within your control—and, therefore, it is your responsibility!

Emotions are a normal, natural part of everyday existence. Emotions are what give each of us meaning in our experience. And, more and more, research suggests that "emotional intelligence" plays a vital role not only in our internal well-being, but in our external success as well.

This doesn't mean that to be successful or live a fulfilling life, you always have to be happy. The idea isn't to limit yourself to only "positive" emotions (joy, elation, euphoria, etc.), but to experiences a full spectrum of emotions, including joy, sorrow, anger, and so much more. That's part of what makes the human experience so rich, complex, and exciting.

Emotions of *any* kind can make you feel more alive, vibrant, and present in your life. (For a counter-example, think of someone who's emotionally distant, disconnected, or shut down—someone who represses their emotions.) Having emotions simply means that you are feeling *something*.

Emotions, like thoughts, aren't permanent. They come and go, passing like clouds that block the sun one moment and dissipate the next. Although some emotions are more pleasant than others (who wouldn't take euphoria over anguish?) there's no need to judge them—and no need to shun the "negative" ones or try to grasp onto the positive ones.

All types of emotions can be messengers and teachers, they can ground you to yourself and connect you with others. They can make you feel more fully alive, more fully human.

Getting in touch with your emotions doesn't require years of psychotherapy, meditation, or introspection. It can be as simple as "checking in with yourself" or asking the basic question, "What's your mood?"

Moods, Weather, and Climate

If moods are like weather, then temperament is like climate.

Someone could have a generally sunny disposition, yet still feel sad from time to time—just like it sometimes rains in the desert. Moods come and go, passing like clouds, but temperament and climate are the overall picture of a person or a place.

Moods are often affected by externals:

- Experiencing a tragedy is likely to make you sad.
- Being wronged can make you angry.
- Taking a walk on a sunny day is likely to bring joy.

...for a while. Ultimately, however, we return to our baseline level of happiness—and all the other emotions that make up our emotional climate.

So, how can you tell if an emotion is just a passing mood or part of your emotional climate? The easiest way is to ask yourself: *Is it recurring?* For example, a rude person might make you angry for a few minutes (or even hours). But if you find yourself stewing over the encounter days later, the anger might have more to do with *you*! Likewise, if you find yourself getting angry on a regular basis over a wide variety of situations and people, the anger might have less to do with the externals than with your internal temperament. In other words, it might be part of your emotional climate.

(This is similar to a phenomenon that frequently shows up in relationships: People might find themselves repeating similar patterns/dynamics in one relationship after another, until they're forced to acknowledge that maybe the issue or "fault" isn't with their various partners, but with themselves.)

The good news is that emotional climates are not immutable. For instance, you *can* raise your baseline level of happiness. You can learn to let go of stress and anger. You can learn to nurture joy and gratitude (a good kind of emotional "global warming"!). It just requires making conscious decisions—beginning with becoming aware of your emotions, accepting responsibility for them, and taking steps to nurture the ones you'd like to grow.

Finances

Financial problems are frequently cited as the leading cause of divorce. In your individual life, money problems can lead to unhappiness, stress, and even serious health problems. On the other hand, free-flowing abundance can

grant you the freedom to spend your time in the most fulfilling manner (instead of working out of necessity—"just for a paycheck"), focus on creative endeavors, and help those in need.

Money is an integral part of self-love. You're not taking very good care of yourself if you relax at the spa for an hour, only to spend the rest of the month stressing about whether or not you can pay your bills! Likewise, you're not helping your romantic life if you feel locked into a relationship merely because you're financially dependent on your partner.

No, money is not the end-all/be-all of life, but it does affect you on many levels. Ignore it at your own peril!

Financial Responsibility and Beliefs about Money

As with other aspects of your life, your personal finances are your responsibility. But perhaps in no other area of life is responsibility more often deflected than with money. It can bring out a person's best (e.g., generosity) or worst (e.g., greed), but it can also bring out a bevy of excuses:

- I didn't come from money.
- The economy is really weak right now.
- No one in my profession has a lot of money.

...and a host of other lines you've probably heard (and/or used yourself) many times—all based on the principle that money (or lack thereof) is beyond your control.

Money can also bring up a host of beliefs—many of which are passed down through the generations, and many of which can be very detrimental to your financial life:

- Money is the root of all evil.
- Having a lot of money means you're superficial and materialistic.
- Only greedy people get rich.

- Rich people can't get into heaven.

You've probably inherited dozens of beliefs about money from your family, peers, and society—perhaps without even being consciously aware of them. Perhaps your family sent the message that you had to struggle tremendously just to get by. Or maybe you learned that money was to be spent rather than saved—that money would "burn a hole in your pocket" if you held onto it for too long. Or maybe you received just the opposite message: that excessive spending is irresponsible, whereas saving is wise and prudent.

Many of the messages and beliefs you've received throughout your life may have been extremely positive and helpful. Nonetheless, part of a conscious life means examining and evaluating these beliefs on your own—and determining for yourself which ones are helping and which ones are hindering your fullest, most joyful experience of life. (Remember: beliefs are self-fulfilling prophecies, so optimistic beliefs about your finances are far more likely to bring you abundance!)

Beliefs are self-fulfilling prophecies!

As with the role of genetics in your physical health, you may not be able to control all of your external circumstances (such as the economy, the financial situation you grew up in, or the messages you were taught about money), but you *can* control your response to these realities—and you can take responsibility for how you live from this point on. And, as with other aspects of life, this process begins with awareness.

Religion, Spirituality, and Faith

Another component of self-fulfillment is your spiritual life. For some people, this might mean being actively affiliated with an organized religion. For others, it might mean pursuing a private spiritual practice. Regardless of what religion and spirituality mean to you, almost everyone can benefit from being involved in something larger than your individual self.

While I don't want to push my beliefs on anyone in this area, I do feel that it can be helpful to get in touch with your *own* beliefs, the experiences that go along with them, and the role of faith in your life.

Faith

Whether or not you consider yourself religious or spiritual, faith probably plays a large role in your life. You might have (or lose) faith in yourself, in another person, or in love.

Faith is what keeps you going through hard times—because you have faith that it will get better. Faith is what allows you to trust a loved one—because you have faith that they want the best for you. Faith in love allows your heart to stay open even after you've been hurt.

But what if you've lost your faith in love?

It's understandable why this might happen. You may have had your heart broken. You may have given love but not received it in return. You may have trusted, only to be betrayed. You may have opened yourself up, made yourself vulnerable, and shared your true self—only to be hit where it hurts most: in your heart!

After such experiences, staying open to love doesn't seem to make any sense. But that's where faith comes in. Not necessarily religious faith (although that can help). Not faith in the people who have hurt you or in your specific experiences—they've taught you that love is painful. Faith in love itself—*that's* what keeps you open.

Faith in love is what keeps you coming back, despite your past, despite the pain. Because somewhere deep within, you feel and believe that love itself is bigger and more powerful than any of the people or experiences that made you want to close up. Because you have faith that love can heal any wound. And because you have faith in yourself—faith that not only can you *experience* a deep love, but that you can *embody* it!

But what if you've lost faith in yourself?

This is the challenge that so many of us face—you stop believing in yourself.

And it's not just about love. You may have lost faith in yourself in other areas: work, diet and exercise, skills and talents, relationships, parenting, money, or almost any other aspect of life—big or small.

Have you ever thought any of these things?:

- I just can't do it.
- It's no use. I've tried and failed—over and over again.
- I've let myself—and others—down too many times.
- I can't be trusted. I can't even trust myself!
- I'm no good.
- I'm a loser.
- I don't deserve any better.
- I can't. I can't. I can't.

If you've ever felt or thought anything like this, you're not alone! Almost everyone gets down on themselves sometimes. Almost everyone has lost faith in themselves at some point.

But, in a weird way, this is good news: it means that you can get it back—just like so many others have done. Just like you may have done—or may be doing right now!

But how do you start? Where do you go to reclaim your faith in yourself? Is there a "Faith Lost and Found"? Actually, yes!

In fact, there are TWO!

Grace

The quickest way to increase and/or regain faith in yourself is through grace—in an instant, you can be filled with faith, with love, with grace. While this may not be entirely within your control, much like falling in love, you can open yourself to it.

If you would like to experience a touch of grace in your own life, take a moment (or however long feels right) to consciously open yourself to grace. Ask for it. Be willing to have your faith restored. Be open to feeling faith in yourself, in love, in your abilities, in others, in the world, in a higher power, or in any other area that you would like to feel more faith and love.

If you would like to, say a prayer, perform a ritual, or even write a letter stating that you are open to having your faith increased through an act of grace. And then wait—with an open heart, mind, and spirit.

Evidence

You can have faith even without evidence, but evidence can always strengthen your faith.

There are three main types of evidence:

- **Experienced Evidence** – Drawn from your own first-hand, personal experiences. For instance, if you have lost faith in your ability to complete a task, look for examples of times when you *have* completed tasks—especially ones that are similar to what you're currently working on. This evidence counteracts your claims or worries that, "I never finish anything! I can't do this!" Yes, you *do* finish things, because you already *have* finished many things! And yes, you *can* do this, because you've already done things that are similar!

- **Borrowed Evidence** – Even if you haven't experienced something first-hand, you can still look for evidence of it in the world around you. For instance, if you've lost your faith in true love, you can look for examples of people who do experience it—even if you haven't. Remember: if *anyone* experiences it, that means you can, too!

- **Created Evidence** – If you simply can't think of any examples of evidence in a particular area—either in your own life or others' lives—then *create* some! Do something that would justify your faith in the area where you want it most!

When you've lost faith in any area of your life—big or small, see if you can find evidence to help you regain it. And if you can't find any, go out and make some! You'll serve as an inspiration to yourself and anyone else who might need a shot of faith in their own lives!

How to "Be the Change"

It's all well and good to think about changes you'd like to make in various areas of your life—to write about them or to talk about them with friends, family, or a counselor—but we all know that making significant change is easier said than done. So how do you actually do it? How do you envision a goal and then actually make it real?

One small step at a time.

This might seem overly simplistic, but it's one of the most important approaches to turning your dreams into reality. So often, people get overly enthusiastic and set unrealistic goals— only to feel disappointed when they fall short. On the other hand, if you take "baby steps" and achieve many micro-successes, you can generally build up enough confidence to move closer and closer to even the loftiest goals.

But planning these baby steps for yourself isn't always enough—you have to be *smart* about it.

Get S.M.A.R.T.

Do you know the acronym S.M.A.R.T.? It's a mnemonic used to help you set goals. There are a number of variations, most of which are along the lines of: **S**pecific, **M**easurable, **A**chievable, **R**ealistic, and **T**imely. You may have seen slightly different words used (including "Evaluate" and "Re-evaluate," which are sometimes added at the end to make it "SMARTER"!), but the main idea is the same. The acronym means that goals (and steps to move toward them) should be clear (not vague or general), and you should know when you plan to reach the goal and what exactly constitutes success.

For instance, if you'd like to write a book, rather than saying, "My goal is to write a lot," you could say, "My goal is to write at least ten pages a week for the next six months."

You can use this approach in almost any area of your life: physical health (e.g., exercising a certain amount of time each week), mental enrichment (e.g., taking a class—a specific step with a clearly delineated goal [to pass the class] within a specific time frame), or even spiritual growth (e.g., praying or meditating a certain amount of time each week).

S.M.A.R.T. Goals

S.M.A.R.T. is an acronym that helps you set effective goals...and reach them! There are numerous variations, most of which are along the lines of:

- Specific
- Measurable
- Achievable
- Realistic
- Timely

Evaluate and Re-evaluate can be added at the end to make it SMARTER!

While growth doesn't always fall neatly within a linear structure, a clear "SMART" goal can get you moving in a positive direction—moving toward miracles, one smart step at a time!

Vision and Evidence

Vision Boards

Another great tool to help you move toward your goals (in any area of life) is a vision board. This is a place where you put pictures that represent your ideal future: a house that you'd like to live in, an ideal partner, your dream vacation spot, or pictures of people embodying qualities you'd like to bring into your life (e.g., joy, enthusiasm, energy)—or anything else that represents your vision of a wonderful life.

A vision board is a great way to dream, envision the life you want, and tap into your youthful, creative, playful side. There's something about searching in magazines, cutting with scissors, and pasting with glue that pulls out a sense of innocence and excitement. Yes, you're participating in an adult exercise of self-fulfillment, but you're also bringing out a beautiful, childlike part of yourself that we adults we so often ignore—letting your inner child out to play!

As much fun as it is to create a vision board, the point isn't just make it and then forget about it, but to look at it regularly (ideally, several times each day). When you look at it, it's very powerful to imagine that you are already living the life it represents—to feel as if these words and images are aspects of your current life. Doesn't that feel great?

A vision board is a wonderful way to reinforce all the positive aspects of the life you're creating. It's not "magic"—it's the power of intention, inner focus, and clear goals. And, most importantly, it actually works! There are countless stories of people successfully using vision boards to bring wonderful people, things, and situations into their lives.

Evidence Boards

Another wonderful tool for creating the life you want is an evidence board. An evidence board is similar to a vision board, except that it uses pictures, words, or any other piece of evidence of things that have *already happened*!

For instance, a person who dreams of going to college might put up a picture of a graduation ceremony on their vision board. A person who has already graduated could put up a picture of him- or herself at their own graduation, holding their diploma—a piece of evidence that they are bright, determined, and able to achieve big goals.

Just imagine the sort of self-confidence boost that a board filled with this sort of evidence could give you if you saw it every day! Imagine how much faith you'd have in yourself if you consistently reinforced such positive self-images! And imagine the drive you'd have to keep adding to it!

Offspring and Propagation

As the old playground song tells us: "First comes love, then comes marriage, then comes the baby in the baby carriage."

Although this is not always the case, it seems that marriage inevitably brings up the topic of children. Oftentimes, no sooner does a couple get married then the questions begin: "So, when are you guys going to have kids?" Or, as commonly phrased by the couple's parents: "When are you going to give me a grandchild?"

This attitude has changed somewhat over the years. These days, many couples decide not to have children. And, on the other hand, many people become single parents by choice.

Regardless of whether or not you're married or have children, the idea of offspring is a very potent symbol for many aspects of every life: creativity, fertility, and new life. You may wish to propagate your ideas and spread your joy, and you probably want to leave a legacy that reflects your highest values. Furthermore, each of us has a tremendous opportunity and responsibility to be a parent to ourselves!

Parenting Yourself

If you are literally a parent, you'd like to set a good example for your children. As easy as it would be to tell them, "Do as I say, not as I do," we all know that children learn by modeling behavior. They learn to speak by listening to their parents and imitating the sounds. They learn how to love by watching the way their parents love. Similarly, they learn how to act, how to treat others, and how to treat themselves by observing the behavior that's modeled for them—largely by their parents.

So, what type of behavior are you modeling for your children? What lessons are you conveying about life, love, and what is and isn't acceptable?

If you don't have children, what example are you setting for the people who are around you? What kind of a role model are you? What are you teaching others through your actions? Or, to look at it another way: what are you teaching yourself? What messages are you sending yourself about the best way to live?

Do your actions send a message that you are valuable—or that it's OK to neglect yourself? Do you treat yourself the way you'd treat your dearest friend? Do you treat yourself the way you'd like to be treated by others? Do you do unto yourself as you would have others do to you? Do you *actively* practice self-love? Are you your own best friend or your own worst enemy?

A Second Chance at Ideal Parenting

How we were raised affects how we see ourselves and our relationships. It affects how we see our inner core worth. In order to be your own best friend and best partner in your life sojourn, you may need to reflect on your upbringing and your parents' role in how you view yourself in the world.

Nobody was raised perfectly. Everybody had moments when they felt like they didn't get enough attention—or they got *too much* attention (or the wrong kind). Everybody had times when they felt like their parents were too strict, too lenient, too smothering, too distant, or too *something*. Maybe you don't feel like your parents were good role models or set good examples. Maybe you feel that they modeled unhealthy behaviors in some ways. Maybe there was something you wanted from them that you didn't get. Or maybe you just wanted something different.

These sorts of feelings and experiences can leave real scars. The good news, however, is that you now have a chance to heal, to make amends, and to get exactly what you want and need—*by giving it to yourself!*

You can't go back in time and change your parents, but YOU can be a parent to yourself right now—the parent who you always wanted! You can "raise" yourself the way you want to be raised—regardless of your age—starting right now!

Creativity and Fertility

Another aspect of children/parenting that extends far beyond literal children is creativity and fertility. This applies to all types of birth, art, and all acts of creation. Indeed, writers, musicians, and other artists often refer to creative surges as a "fertile period." And it's true, many creative projects can feel like the stages of birth:

- **Conception** – The initial spark, the moment when an idea or a project is conceived.

- **Gestation and Growth** – The time when a project grows in private, nurtured in a "womb" of creativity.

- **Birth** – The moment when the creative project is shared with the outside world, when the private becomes public.

- **A Life of Its Own** – Books, movies, and other creative projects generally take on "a life of their own" after they are released—sometimes short-lived, sometimes being received very differently from how their "parent" intended.

- **Breaks from Pregnancy/Birth** – While some artists seem to create continuously (just as some women become pregnant almost immediately after giving birth), it is more common to have fallow periods—which can greatly enhance future creativity (and help maintain a sense of balance in the artist/parent's life).

- **Future Children** – When an artist produces multiple works, they may be similar to one another (bear a "family resemblance") or look nothing alike—representing disparate aspects of their creator.

My mother frequently says that she's so impressed that I scrapbook and write, and that my daughter and her cousins are so artistic. Yet she's somehow convinced herself that she isn't artistic, that it just isn't in her genetic makeup. I have to laugh and respond, "Where do you think we all got our artistic talent from?" But she never even attempts to build her artistic muscles. She's just so convinced that she doesn't have any artistic talent, that she never tries. She never grants herself the freedom of unrestricted artistic play; but I have a feeling that, if she did, she'd amaze herself at what she was able to create!

Regardless of whether you're a painter, writer, chef, entrepreneur, or a literal parent—you ARE an artist! We all create! We all bring something new into the world.

Values and Legacy

Two final aspects of children that apply to all of us—whether or not we have literal children—are passing on our values and leaving a legacy.

All of us wish to share our values. Some people do it by teaching their kids the "right" way to live. Some people do it by writing letters to the editor sharing their viewpoints. Others do it by trying to set a good example through how they live their own lives.

The values that we pass along—to children and/or anyone else who we touch with our lives—is part of our legacy, our bequest, what we leave the world. This also includes our works, the impact we had on other people and our environment, as well as the love and energy that we shared throughout our lives. If we are a stone thrown in the pool of life, our legacy is the ripples. How do you want your "ripples" to affect people after you're gone?

The rest of your life begins NOW!

Take some time to reflect on the various aspects of your daily life—from your thoughts, emotions, and physical health to your personal and the legacy you're creating. Just like most of a marriage is made up of small, everyday activities, so is your individual life. And these details add up—moment by moment, day by day, year by year—to make you who you are.

~ EXERCISES ~

Secondary Gains

What physical and/or emotional ailments have you experienced recently? What are some possible secondary gains from these ailments?_____

_____

_____

_____

_____

Do any of these ailments reflect messages you received while growing up (e.g., the body starts "falling apart" after you reach a certain age, winter is "flu season," or osteoporosis [or some other ailment] runs in our family)? _____

_____

_____

_____

_____

How might you be able to receive similar (or better) gains without the ailment?_____

_____

_____

_____

_____

*What are some potential benefits of taking full responsibility for your health—and experiencing physical/holistic vitality?*_____

_____

_____

_____

_____

Physical Health

The Health Wheel

Part of taking full responsibility for your health is taking a clear-eyed look at various aspects of your present health. The "Health Wheel" is a "snapshot" evaluation designed to help you do just that. It is something that I offer my patients to make sure they're not overtly neglecting any important aspect of their physical health.

If you shade in your level of health (rating yourself from 1-10) in each of the major categories, you'll be able to get a snapshot of the areas where you could most benefit from additional attention. (E.g., maybe you exercise and maintain a healthy weight, but don't sleep enough or drink enough water.) Your goal is to have a 10 in all areas so that your "wheel" of life rolls smoothly.

Fill in your level of health in each of the major areas.

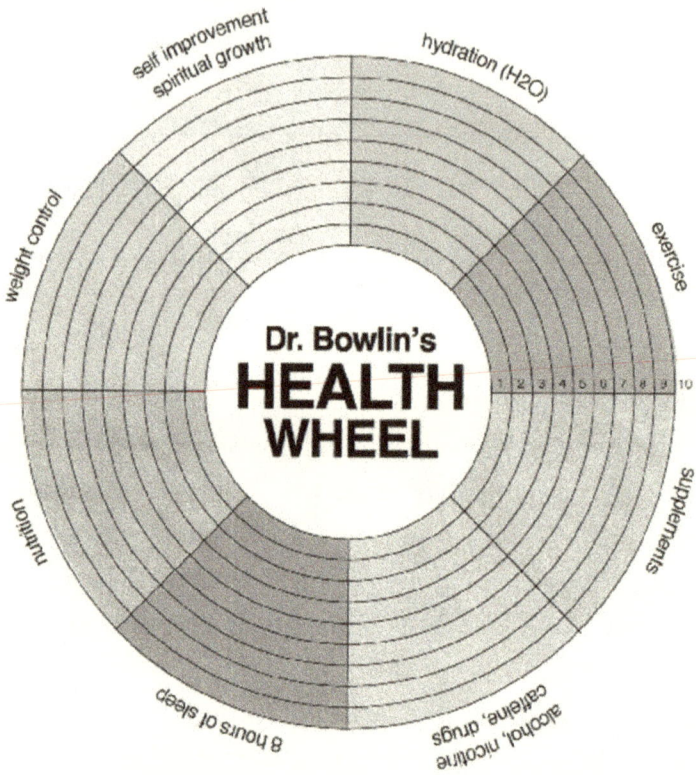

Dr. Bowlin's
HEALTH
WHEEL

self improvement spiritual growth · hydration (H2O) · exercise · supplements · alcohol, nicotine caffeine, drugs · 8 hours of sleep · nutrition · weight control

1 2 3 4 5 6 7 8 9 10

What did you learn from filling out the Health Wheel? _____

_____

_____

_____

_____

_____

_____

_____

_____

_____

_____

What steps would you like to take to help you maintain more vibrant, holistic health? (E.g., You might schedule your exercise into your daily or weekly plan, just as if it were a business appointment, or you might stock the house with healthy snacks.)

_____

_____

_____

_____

_____

Mental Hygiene

What are your favorite ways to keep your mind sharp and feed your intellect (e.g., crossword puzzles, stimulating conversations, thought-provoking books)? _____

_____

_____

Is there anything you'd like to do—or do more of—to keep your mind sharp (e.g., learn a new language or the latest technology)?

_____

_____

_____

On a scale of 1-10, how optimistic do you consider yourself? _____

How does this optimism (or lack thereof) show up in your life, and how does it affect you? _____

_____

_____

Is there anything you'd like to do—or do more of—to increase your level of optimism? How do you think you might benefit from this?

_____

_____

_____

_____

_____

Emotional Awareness

Do you certain emotions tend to show up at predictable times/events in your life? _____

What are you generally like (emotionally) in the morning? _____

_____

_____

In the afternoon? _____

_____

_____

At night? _____

_____

_____

What are you like when your spouse and/or children get home (or when you come home to them—or come home to an empty house)?

_____

_____

*What are some other situations in which you have predictable emotional responses?*_____

_____

_____

*Aside from short-term ups and downs, how would you summarize your emotional "climate"?*_____

_____

_____

_____

How often do you experience the following emotions, and in what situations do they tend to arise?

Happiness: _____

_____

Sadness: _____

_____

Anger: _____

_____

*Anxiety/Stress:*_____

_____

Peacefulness/Serenity: _____

_____

(Others): _____

_____

How do you get in touch with your emotions and express them in healthy ways? What are steps you could take to become even more emotionally healthy (e.g., exercising, meditating, or practicing other stress-reduction techniques)? _____

_____

_____

_____

Have you ever blamed other people and/or external events for your emotional reactions, only to notice those emotions recurring again and again in your own life (apart from those externals)? If so, what were the emotions and situations in which you felt them?

_____

_____

_____

On a scale of 1-10, how would you rate your baseline happiness (i.e., how happy you typically are under normal conditions)? ____

Would you like to raise your baseline happiness and/or make any other changes in your emotional climate? If so, what? _____

_____

_____

_____

_____

What are three steps that you could take to start this process?

_____

_____

_____

~~~~~~

Financial Awareness

Write down all of the words and phrases that you associate with money: _____

_____

_____

_____

_____

Are there any more positive words that you'd like to associate with money? How do you think that these positive associations might help improve your financial situation? _____

_____

_____

_____

_____

How satisfied are you with your current financial situation (on a scale of 1-10)? ____

If you answered anything other than a 10, what are some steps that you can take to move you closer to a 10? _____

_____

_____

_____

_____

_____

_____

_____

_____

*How educated are you about financial matters (from 1-10)?*_____

*What are some steps that you can take to become more educated about finances (e.g., visit a financial advisor, take a class, or read a book about finances)?*_____

_____

_____

_____

What steps might help you with the following area of your finances?

*Earning:*_____

_____

Saving: _____

_____

Spending: _____

_____

*Planning (e.g., retirement fund):*_____

_____

Investments: _____

_____

Bookkeeping: _____

_____

(Others): _____

_____

Your Spiritual Beliefs and Practices

*What are your primary spiritual/religious beliefs?*_____

_____

_____

_____

_____

_____

_____

_____

_____

_____

What spiritual and/or religious practices do you do on a regular basis? _____

_____

_____

_____

_____

*Are there any steps you'd like to take to create a more fulfilling spiritual/religious life (e.g., join a community, meditate or pray more often, or learn about different spiritual paths)?*_____

_____

_____

_____

_____

~~~~~~
Faith

Whether or not you've lost faith in yourself, you can almost always benefit from more! Healthy faith in yourself—just like healthy self-esteem, self-confidence, and self-worth—is one of the greatest assets for every aspect of your life.

The questions and exercises below can help you get in touch with your own level of faith, regain lost faith, and restore your confidence in yourself, in love, and in life.

Areas of Faith

Think of the major areas of your life: self-love, relationships, work, and the areas discussed above (health, finances, etc.). How much faith do you have in each area? Where do you feel the most faith? Where do you feel the least? _____

_____

_____

_____

_____

_____

*In the areas where you have the least faith, what evidence can you think of to bolster your faith? (Remember, the evidence can come from your own life or from others' lives.)*_____

_____

_____

_____

_____

_____

What steps can you take to **create** more evidence—and bolster your faith in yourself? _____

_____

_____

_____

_____

_____

SMART Goals

What are some goals—in any area of your life—that you might like to pursue in the near future? _____

_____

_____

_____

_____

_____

If you had to focus on just one of these goals, which one would it be? _____

What is one small step that you could take to move you toward this goal? (Make sure that it fits the "SMART" criteria!) _____

_____

_____

_____

_____

_____

Create a Vision Board and an Evidence Board

Make your own Vision Board

Using a bulletin board or poster board, put up pictures, words, memorabilia, or anything that represents aspects of your ideal life.

*What are some words or images you might include on your vision board?*_____

_____

_____

_____

Make your own Evidence Board

*As with your vision board, put up pictures/words that provide evidence of your positive qualities, achievements, or any experience that increases your faith in yourself—and gives you a boost toward the future you want! What are some words, images, or memorabilia (e.g., diplomas, certificates) you might include on your evidence board?*_____

_____

_____

_____

_____

From Vision to Evidence

After you've created both boards, one of the most gratifying experiences is when you can take an image off of your vision board and transfer it to your evidence board—a sign that your dreams are becoming reality!

Lessons from Your Parents, Lessons from Yourself

*What lessons did your parents' behavior convey about love, relationships, self-care, and other important aspects of life?*_____

_____

_____

_____

_____

_____

What lessons do you wish they had conveyed? _____

_____

_____

_____

_____

*How would a parent act if they wished to convey these messages? How would they embody these lessons?*_____

_____

_____

_____

_____

*What can you do in your life right now so that you embody these messages—teaching by example—for yourself and others?*_____

_____

_____

_____

_____

_____

Your Creative "Children"

What are some things that you've created in your life? (They don't have to be examples of literal, tangible art or actual children— they could be anything new that you've brought into the world, such as a business project or a new recipe).

_____

_____

_____

_____

Describe your creative process: _____

_____

_____

_____

Have you experienced any parallels to the process of having actual children (e.g., a gestation period, a painful birth, or pride in your "progeny")? _____

_____

_____

When have you felt the most creatively "fertile"? (A certain time of the year? A certain day of the week or time of the day?) _____

_____

_____

What are some steps you can take to nurture your creativity? _____

_____

_____

_____

Clarifying and Passing on Your Values and Legacy

Before you pass on your values or leave a legacy, it helps to clarify what your values are. What do you hold in the highest regard, cherish the most, consider most valuable? _____

_____

_____

_____

_____

_____

_____

_____

*If you had only a few minutes to live and you had your children (and/or closest friends/family) with you, what would you tell them? What if you could speak to the entire world? What would you say as your final words? (Be as succinct as possible—see if you can express your core message in just 1-2 sentences.)*_____

_____

_____

_____

_____

_____

_____

What would you like your legacy to be? _____

_____

_____

_____

_____

*If you died today, what would your legacy actually be?*_____

_____

_____

_____

_____

*What would you have to do to make your above two answers the same (if they're not already)?*_____

_____

_____

_____

_____

Happily Ever After?

Yes, it would be wonderful to live happily ever after, but what happens when the road gets bumpy? How do you overcome the obstacles life presents? How do you know when to persevere and when to call it quits? And if you do feel separated—from yourself, from others, or from life—how do you reconnect? How do you *return to yourself*?

Chapter Eight

Challenges, Separation,

And Return

~ *Overcoming Obstacles and Coming Back to Yourself* ~

How many times have you seen it happen: two celebrities fall in love, embark on a whirlwind romance culminating in a glamorous, million-dollar wedding— every moment of which is covered (and scrutinized' *ad nauseum*) on TV, online, and in every supermarket tabloid—and they end up divorced before the next news cycle.

Sometimes the glamorous couples actually make it to the one-year mark—and occasionally even to seven (which seems to be the breaking—or "itching"—point for many couples). In Hollywood terms, 10 years of marriage is an eon and a half! It's the rare exception that actually stays together for life.

Why is this? Why is it that two successful, accomplished, rich, and in most cases preternaturally beautiful people have such a hard time staying together? They have fame, fortune, love, and each other—what could possibly be the problem?

While every couple is different, I would venture to guess that the issue is exactly what we've been talking about throughout this entire book:

Fantasy vs. Reality

This issue affects us all, but it's compounded when the people involved are celebrities. It's so easy to get caught up in the on-stage or on-screen persona: the action hero, the goddess, the rock star, the diva, the comedian...in short, the image, the illusion, the fantasy.

But the person who they find themselves married to isn't the character who jumps his motorcycle over a moving train, rocks a stadium packed with adoring fans, or seduces the spy while delivering witty double entendres—it's the real-life person who wakes up grumpy because they have a kink in their neck, got a bad night's sleep, and are out of coffee. In other words: a human being.

But it's not just celebrities who are susceptible to this fantasy trap. Roughly half of all marriages in the U.S. end in divorce. And although many reasons are provided (financial problems, infidelity, irreconcilable differences, or just a good old-fashioned rut), it seems safe to say that the underlying cause for most break-ups is the same: he/she/life didn't turn out to be the way I thought/hoped they would. In other words: *the reality didn't match the fantasy.*

You don't have to be a movie star to get caught up in fantasy. You don't have to be dating a celebrity to project your ideals onto someone, lose yourself in starry-eyed romance, and dream of a fairytale wedding.

Not that there's anything wrong with wanting—or having—a fairytale wedding. It's wonderful to celebrate the joining of two lives and two hearts. It's important to honor the love of a lifetime. And it's beautiful to share this occasion with the people dearest to you.

It's also important to remember one critical point:

The wedding is one day; marriage is for the rest of your life.

(At least half the time.)

The balance of focus, time, attention, and money doesn't always reflect this, however; many people spend so much time planning their weddings that it consumes them—it becomes a full-time job, an obsession. In addition to the time spent, the cost of those few hours (the ring, the dress, the food, the venue, etc., etc., etc.) can be one of the biggest expenses of their lives— sometimes more than a down payment for a house would be!

Again, there's nothing wrong with big, fancy weddings. I'm not suggesting that everyone get married at town hall and put the saved money toward a practical family sedan—any more than I'm suggesting that husbands buy their wives appliances as anniversary presents. Flowers, however impractical, are always welcome. Romance and even occasional extravagance can be wonderful—the sort of experiences and memories that can warm the heart for a lifetime. Weddings can be beautiful highlights of a lifetime of love—as long as people keep things in perspective and remember that this is merely a celebration of the love that they will be sharing for years to come.

Much of the time, however, after the build-up of the planning, the excitement of the wedding itself, and the pleasure of the honeymoon, many people experience a letdown when they go back to their regular lives. It's no surprise that the phrase "the honeymoon is over" is used in contexts far beyond literal marriages and honeymoons—usually spoken with a tone of wistful cynicism.

So, what does this mean for you as an individual?

Whether you're married or not, these experiences can teach us all a lot about our individual lives—especially regarding short-term vs. long-term focus, projection, and letdowns.

Short Term vs. Long Term

Focusing more on your individual wedding day than on the entirety of your married life is a perfect example of a common tendency: choosing short-term excitement over long-term commitment.

Have you ever fallen into this trap? Have you ever felt excitement about a new project, only to watch it fizzle out as the reality of the long-term work began to sink in? Have you given in to the allure of instant gratification rather than the lasting rewards of delayed gratification?

Or are you on the opposite end of the spectrum? Do you tend toward joy postponement? Do you procrastinate? Do you put off rewards, focus primarily on the future, and neglect to enjoy the here-and-now?

Do you focus more on the "wedding day" (literally and/or figuratively) or on the "marriage"?

Projection

Projection is another one of the biggest traps people fall into—in all areas of life. It can mean projecting your highest ideals or your worst fears onto someone. In either case, however, you're not seeing the other person for who they truly are.

You're not experiencing reality.

It often happens when people idealize a new boyfriend, girlfriend, or spouse; but it doesn't just apply to romantic situations. People can idealize a friend, demonize a boss, or even fool themselves into thinking that they are very different from the way they really are.

It's understandable why people do this: we all hope for the best. We hope that the new person we've just met is Ms. or Mr. Right. We want this job we've applied for to be our dream job— the one that ends our struggles and finally brings us satisfaction and security. We don't want to admit to—or even see—the flaws in our best friends (or in ourselves).

In short, we prefer our fantasies over reality.

But reality has a way of catching up with you. "Mr. Right" drinks too much. The new "dream job" turns out to be even more stressful (or boring, unfulfilling, etc.) than the last one. Or that person you've demonized for so long ends up doing some very nice, selfless favors for you—and you're forced to admit that perhaps you were too hasty in your judgment. Eventually, cognitive dissonance becomes strong enough that you have to adjust your perception of reality to match the world beyond your mind.

And this is a good thing.

We don't want to live a lie. We don't want to go through life believing that things are very different from how they actually are—even when that belief is temporarily comforting. We want to wake up to reality.

And when we do this, we realize something amazing: reality can be even more wonderful than fantasy. Reality is rich and beautiful and stimulating and challenging and varied and complex and, ultimately, more satisfying than any dream or projection.

Also, "facing reality" does not mean that your life can't have peak moments of profound beauty, magic, and romance. It simply means that it is more—*so much more*—than these peak moments. It is the peak moments *plus* everything else! Reality is the crest of the wave plus the entire ocean. Reality is the night of passion as well as the next morning. Reality is the courtship, the engagement, the wedding, the honeymoon, *and* everything afterwards.

And you can savor all of it.

Letdown

After a wedding, there can be a sense of relief—a sense of "Whew, we did it!" After all the planning and excitement and drama (which often increases exponentially when two separate families are thrown into the mix)—you can finally exhale, relax, and enjoy the return to normal life.

There can also be a letdown.

Many people see their whole life as a build-up to this moment, and now it's done. Yes, you're moving on to other things, other exciting adventures and opportunities, but this big (for some people, the biggest) one is now over.

It's understandable that you might feel some sadness. So, rather than berating yourself and thinking about all of the things you "should" be thinking and feeling (excitement at starting a new phase of life, the joy of marital bliss, etc.), allow yourself to think and feel exactly what you're experiencing—without judgment or expectation.

The same holds true for the aftermath of any major event, experience, or accomplishment. Even when it is successful (perhaps *especially* when it's successful), you can feel a letdown afterwards.

> ***There are only two tragedies in life:***
> *one is not getting what one wants, and the other is getting it.*
> *~ Oscar Wilde*

As Oscar Wilde famously quipped, "There are only two tragedies in life: one is not getting what one wants, and the other is getting it."

While the first part of this statement is universally acknowledged (everyone wishes to attain their desires), there's also truth to the second half. In some cases, the object of your desire (a spouse, a new job, a new home, or any other goal attained) fails to live up to your hopes. (Again, the fantasy trap!) Even if it does live up to your hopes, however, it can still leave you feeling let down. After all, getting what you want can be disorienting. Suddenly, after months or years of working toward a goal, it's done. The object that you'd been moving toward for so long is now behind you. This can leave you feeling directionless, without a purpose. You may feel empty.

(This may even be a reason why people sometimes sabotage their own goals: they sense—perhaps subconsciously—that their lives would lack direction or purpose if they did attain their goals.)

This is not to suggest, however, that we *should* sabotage our goals. It would be silly to intentionally flunk out of school with only half a semester until graduation. It would be ludicrous to turn down a financial windfall just because we wouldn't know what to do with ourselves if we weren't constantly scrambling for money. And, to return to our central metaphor, we shouldn't turn down a marriage proposal from our ideal partner simply because that would leave us unable to continue *seeking* the love of our life—or bemoaning our depressing lack of a love life.

It's also not necessarily advisable to rush headlong into a new project—chasing another "carrot" the moment after we've reached the last one. The healthiest approach is probably to celebrate an accomplishment, recognize a milestone, and savor the moment—and then allow yourself some time to reorient. Simply *be* in your new position. Experience it for what it is. Let yourself feel your feelings—even if they aren't what you'd hoped or expected they would be. Allow yourself to be in the "in-between" space. Consider new perspectives and possibilities without feeling compelled to immediately take action. Allow yourself to simply be.

The Blame Game

After the honeymoon is over (literally or figuratively) problems commonly and inevitably arise. Sometimes these problems are small and short-lived, other times they're serious and ongoing. And sometimes, if not addressed, minor disagreements can turn into chronic nagging arguments—which can pop up in many different forms, although they generally stem from the same underlying themes and issues.

When frustration and disagreements show up in a relationship, the first instinct for many people is to blame their partners. Have you ever thought, said, or heard someone else say any of the following:

- You never listen to me.
- He's just not willing to compromise.
- She's being unreasonable.
- How could you do this to me?

...or any similar accusations? All of the above complaints (and their infinite variations) have the same core message:

It's not my fault!

If only my partner would change! If only they would admit the error of their ways! If only they would take responsibility! If only they would realize that I'm right and they're wrong!

Yes, oftentimes you may indeed be right. More often than not, however, situations have (at least) two sides—and many shades of gray. But rather than recognize these shades, consider another perspective, or take personal responsibility for problems, many couples get caught up in the blame game.

This pernicious "game" tears at the fabric of a relationship. It can turn a loving partnership into a vitriolic competition. It shifts the focus from building each other up to tearing each other down. And when that happens, both sides lose.

Perhaps worst of all, the blame game removes the power of the blamer. Saying that a problem is someone (or something) else's fault means that you don't have the need or the power, knowledge or skill to fix it. Blaming others for your unhappiness means that you freely give up responsibility for your own life. After all, if you have no control over the problem, how can you bring about a solution? And if you have no power to bring about a solution, you fall into the trap of "learned helplessness"—and the depression that comes from perceived inability to affect one's situation.

So, does this mean that instead of blaming others, that you should beat yourself up? Not at all. That's just changing from "The Blame Game" to "The Shame Game."

Shame is another way of letting yourself get off the hook: If you go around saying what a terrible person you are, then you don't have to stop being terrible, right? (You can also expect other people to rush to your defense: "No, no—you're not terrible. You're such a good person!") If you punish yourself, then you don't have to change your behavior. If you say that you're a bad person, then you've made the condition permanent rather than something within your control, something that you can change.

The Secondary Gains of Blame and Shame

Remember "Bob"—my patient with the chronic nasal congestion complaints? Well, just like he had secondary gains from his congestion (such as attention, social interaction, and physical contact), we all get secondary benefits when we blame others or shame ourselves. We avoid the hard, lonely work of self-examination. We avoid the need to change ourselves. And we get to deny our role in causing problems in a relationship.

But what if the relationship in question is your relationship with yourself? In this case the bad news is that there's no one else to blame. But this is also the good news, because it means that *you* have the power to change the situation—the "relationship." And this forces you to learn perhaps the most important lesson of your entire life:

Personal Responsibility

Taking responsibility for your experiences—rather than blaming externals—is the most empowering step you can take in your life. Whether you're dealing with physical health, emotions, finances, relationships, or any aspect of your personal well-being, responsibility is the key to self-love.

Taking responsibility is a sign of maturity. Immature people say: "I can't help it! He made me do it! It's not my fault!" Mature people say: "The buck stops here!" Immature people blame, complain, and whine. Mature people accept their present reality, acknowledge their role in creating it, and take proactive steps to move closer to their ideal lives. People living in shame say to themselves, "I'm a bad person, I'm too embarrassed, I can never truly be myself." Mature people forgive themselves, learn from their mistakes, and share their shortcomings with others so that others may also learn from those mistakes (and hopefully avoid them).

A Sign of Maturity

Remember, however, that responsibility is about your own personal experience. It doesn't mean that you're responsible for other people or that you can control all the external circumstances of your life. What you can control, however, is your response to them.

Remember the "response-ability" concept that we've talked about? We considered that you always have the ability to choose your response—including when you feel a spark of romantic potential. Well, you also have the ability to choose your response when sparks fly in unpleasant ways! For instance, you can't control whether or not someone yells at you, and you can't necessarily stop yourself from getting angry—but you *can* control whether you yell back or take steps to diffuse the situation.

This "response-ability" principle is even more powerful in your relationship with yourself, and it affects nearly every part of your life. It always presents you with a choice between relinquishing your personal power (playing the blame game) or embracing your personal power (taking responsibility). Even if that means forgiving others and yourself of significant, emotionally painful trespasses. Even if that means letting go of the secondary gains of victimhood. Even if that means growing and moving on.

Of course, while responsibility is a great foundation for personal growth and moving toward your ideal life, it doesn't guarantee that problems won't arise. In your relationship with yourself, just as in literal marriages, sometimes you need a little extra help getting through the rocky parts.

Couples' Counseling...for Individuals

Sometimes, despite our best efforts to have a strong marriage, to be good parents, to take personal responsibility, and to live our best lives as individuals, difficulties arise. Unexpected challenges threaten our peace of mind: a partner is unfaithful, we have financial problems, or we just get stuck in a rut.

Some of the most common concerns that arise in couples' counseling sessions—and threaten to break up marriages—can apply equally to any of us on an individual level. Let's look at some of them, and explore ways to address them...before they break you up!

Infidelity

Infidelity is one of the most serious challenges that a couple can face. It is, in some ways, the ultimate betrayal. It erodes trust, confidence, and love—and is often the undoing of a relationship.

"But how does infidelity relate to me as an individual?" you might wonder. Well, even if you're not in a relationship—or if you are in a 100% monogamous one—you can still ask yourself:

- Am I faithful to myself?

- Do I keep my promises to others?

- Do I keep my word to myself?

- Am I true to my core values and my highest ideals?

- Am I trustworthy?

Just as you would presumably want a partner whom you could trust, you want to be able to trust yourself. You don't want to violate the trust that you put in yourself. You want your actions to reflect your values. You *don't* want your actions to betray yourself.

In a relationship, sexual and/or emotional infidelity is generally the outward symptom of a deeper issue, such as feeling dissatisfied or unappreciated. It can also be a very clear signal that maybe your partner isn't "The One" for you!

If you can look beyond the emotional pain of betrayal, you might be able to see that this hurtful act could save you decades of an unsatisfying relationship—and open the door to something better. The same could hold true for an individual: If you notice yourself "betraying" your values, perhaps it's a sign that your values and/or priorities have changed.

Consider one meaning of the word "betray": *to reveal or expose*—as in "He tried not to gloat, but his smile betrayed his joy at the victory." Perhaps the "betrayal" is actually a revelation of a deeper truth, one that may have been hidden even to yourself.

Becoming aware of your *true* feelings, inclinations, and interests can be an extremely valuable wake-up call!

Exercise: Individual Infidelity

Am I trustworthy? Do I keep my word to myself and others?
*Imagine, for instance, that you have a lunch date set up each week with a friend, and week after week that friend does not show up but you do. Will you trust that friend and have faith in her commitment? Have you ever been that friend who doesn't show up week after week to your commitments—to eat better, to exercise, to take better care of yourself? If so, have you lost faith and trust in yourself?*_____

_____

_____

_____

_____

_____

_____

*What would it look like if I were completely faithful to myself—if I always showed up for myself? What would I accomplish? How would I feel?*_____

_____

_____

_____

_____

Finances

As mentioned earlier, money issues are often cited as the leading cause of divorce. Even if couples do stay together through their financial struggles, these problems can create tremendous stress, which often spills over into other areas of a relationship. Also, partners might have different approaches and attitudes toward money (e.g., one of them is a big spender, the other likes to save for the future), which can cause friction.

Whether you're married or single, it can be very helpful to you as an individual to clarify your own financial goals and attitudes. Also, learning the basics of finances can empower you and make it less likely that you'll get into an unhealthy relationship simply because you feel you need someone to take care of you. Financial independence can help you stand on your own two feet—and be an equal partner if you're in a relationship.

∿∿

Exercise: Money and Me

Complete this sentence: Money is _____

_____

Beliefs about Money

*What beliefs about money did you grow up with—in your family, peer group, etc.? (E.g., Were you taught that money was the "root of all evil," that it was the key to freedom and happiness, or that it was unimportant?) How do your current beliefs differ?*_____

_____

_____

_____

_____

Money Habits

*What are your current money habits? Do you enjoy spending money? Saving money? Do you feel the need to acquire many things, or are you happier living simply?*_____

_____

_____

_____

_____

_____

_____

_____

_____

Financial Goals

What are your financial goals, and how do you plan on reaching them? _____

_____

_____

_____

_____

_____

_____

_____

_____

Sex

Sex is one of the only things that set apart platonic relationships from marriage and other non-platonic relationships.

- You're very close with your spouse—but you're also close with your best friends.

- Your spouse knows you very well—but so does your family.

- You spend a lot of time with your spouse—but you also spend lots of time with co-workers.

But when you're in a monogamous relationship, sex is something you only share with your partner. It can be a source of tremendous pleasure and love—bringing you closer, providing a way to connect deeply and intimately, a way for you to express your love and passion for one another.

However, it can also be a source of disharmony for some couples.

Whether you're married or single, sex can be a very sensitive topic—one which you might find difficult to talk about or even consider. That is why it's especially important for you to understand your *own* views, experiences, hopes, and expectations about sex. Once you're clear about your own thoughts, it will hopefully be easier to communicate with a spouse or other sex partner—either now or in the future.

Exercise: S-E-X

What does sex mean to you? _____

_____

_____

_____

_____

_____

What beliefs about sex did you grow up with—in your family, peer group, etc.? (E.g., Were you taught that sex is dirty and sinful, or that it is a healthy part of a loving relationship?) How do your current beliefs differ? _____

_____

_____

_____

_____

_____

_____

_____

What were your earliest experiences with sex? How did they shape your current view and experience of sex?_____

_____

_____

_____

_____

_____

_____

What does your ideal sex life look like? _____

_____

_____

_____

_____

_____

_____

_____

Who would your ideal sex partner be (either a real person or an imagined ideal)? What about them appeals to you? _____

_____

_____

_____

_____

_____

_____

_____

Do you have any sexual difficulties, hang-ups, insecurities, or other issues that might get in the way of experiencing a healthy sex life? If so, how might you be able to address these issues? _____

_____

_____

_____

_____

_____

_____

_____

Communication

One of the most common complaints that marriage counselors (and many others) hear is, "He/She never *listens* to me"—or variations thereof: "You're not *hearing* what I'm saying," "Why didn't you ever *tell* me about this?" or "I wish you would *communicate* better!"

It's accepted as a self-evident truth that communication is the key to a good relationship. And this doesn't just apply to marriages. Effective communication at work can make the difference between getting a promotion and getting fired. Effective communication with your children can help them grow into confident, successful adults. Effective communication with those around you on a day-to-day basis can make the difference between developing close, meaningful connections and drifting through life feeling lonely, disconnected, and shut off from the world around you.

But why would we discuss communication in a book about individuals? Because no matter who you're communicating with, there's always one common variable: YOU!

Exercise: Communication Skills

Do you think other people would consider you a good listener? ____

*Is there any comment/criticism about your communication skills that you've heard more than once? What is it?*_____

_____

_____

_____

*Describe your self-talk. In other words, how do you talk to yourself (in your head)? Are you generally critical and harsh on yourself, or are you encouraging and nourishing? What are some things that you notice yourself thinking/telling yourself often?*_____

_____

_____

_____

_____

*Where and when do you think you picked up these habits? (For instance, did you hear one parent berate another—or themselves? When did you decide that it was OK to talk to put yourself down? Or, on the positive side, did you have any good role models who showed you what it was like to build yourself up in healthy ways?)*_

_____

_____

_____

_____

HOMEWORK:
Improving how you communicate with others reflects how you communicate with yourself. By practicing exercises of improved communication and active listening, you'll build personal restraint and improved understanding of yourself and others. Here are three communication exercises to try with others:

Mirroring
You may have heard of this technique, where you listen to someone and then paraphrase their words back to them in order to make sure you're hearing what they're saying. Try this with a partner or friend, letting them know you'd like to try it first (so they don't

wonder why you're talking funny, saying things like, "What I'm hearing you say is...". It can be useful in many situations—even at work (like a waiter or waitress repeating back your order to make sure they've gotten it right). It might feel awkward at first, but the more you do this, the more natural it will feel. This will help you clarify and eliminate frequent miscommunication.

Don't Interrupt!

This may seem too obvious to mention, but the next time you're having a conversation (of any kind), be aware of letting the other person finish. Don't jump in, interrupt, or try to finish their sentences for them. First of all, you might not know what they're going to say! Secondly, interruption shows disrespect as well as impatience. It also shows you are truly not listening actively. Thirdly, even when a person is angry, oftentimes all they want is a chance to speak their piece. It's amazing how often simply letting them say what they want to say—without being interrupted (especially in a defensive way)—is enough to satisfy someone.

Just Listen

Perhaps most importantly of all, when you're listening to someone, really listen! Don't just be thinking of what you're going to say, waiting to jump in as soon as they're finished—especially if it's to tell them why you're right and they're wrong! Actually take in what they're saying. Practice being receptive. The other person will feel heard and validated—and they'll be much more likely to respect and listen to you when it is your turn to speak. It's amazing how much you can learn when you actively listen to someone without running your internal thought processes about what your planning to say next.

Stuck in a Rut

While couples' counselors hear many dramatic complaints—about problems ranging from infidelity to abusiveness—oftentimes it's the more mundane issues that can erode a relationship...or an individual's happiness and well-being. Perhaps the most common issue of this type is feeling that your marriage—or your life—is simply stuck in a rut.

The good news is that this doesn't have to be a permanent condition. Everyone falls into ruts from time to time. The trick is learning to recognize them, get out of them, and get back on a healthier track.

Exercise: Getting Unstuck

Do you feel stuck in any area of your life (at work, at home, with your children, with your finances, or with your life in general)? If so, how? If not, when was the last time you did feel this way?

_____

_____

_____

_____

_____

*When (and in what ways) have you felt a sense of FLOW (the opposite of stuck)?*_____

_____

_____

_____

_____

What are some ways you might be able to make yourself "unstuck"? Do you think you need to drop some externals (activities, relationships, etc.) that no longer fit you, try something new, shift your internal perspective (e.g., focusing on gratitude rather than problems)—or all of the above? Describe one or two specific steps you can try that might create a greater sense of flow in your life. _____

_____

_____

_____

_____

As much as you might love to always resolve difficulties and overcome challenges, sometimes marriages break up. Sometimes, the obstacles are just too big to overcome. Or sometimes, perhaps over the course of many years, you just drift away from each other—or from yourself.

What do you do when separation occurs? How do you get back on track? Even if a marriage ends, how do you get *yourself* back?

My Separation

That first morning I woke up alone in my new house, I was amazed at what I heard: absolutely nothing.

After a decade of waking up 3-10 times per night—either because of my children, my husband's snoring, or our emergency pagers going off—I had actually slept straight through until morning!

The silence was like a revelation.

I could think! I could reflect on my situation—without the cobwebs of sleep deprivation cluttering my head. I could try to piece together what had led to this separation.

It had happened gradually.

I was so grateful to have a loving, caring husband that I didn't want to sabotage it (as I'd done with past relationships). I figured that things would be smoother if I just went along with him— didn't rock the boat, didn't express my true feelings.

It started with little things (where to hang a painting), grew to medium-sized choices (how many cats to get), and eventually affected major life decisions (where to live).

None of this was malicious. Far from it—I knew that my husband always wanted the best for me. He wanted so strongly to be my protector, to help me with my fears and all the newness surrounding me. He wanted to be my knight in shining armor, saving me from all my inner dangerous threats.

And I was more than happy to oblige. I felt that I needed such a strong individual in my life—so much so that I lost much of myself in the process. I respected him and his judgments and believed in him so much that I stopped being autonomous. Rather than assert myself, I got in the habit of yielding to my husband's agenda.

By denying my own wants, needs, desires, and opinions, I thought I was being a good wife. Little did I realize that I was slowly building resentment. My inability to speak up and set healthy boundaries was chipping away at my self-esteem. Over the course of many years—over a decade of not speaking my truth—I lost more than just my voice: I lost myself.

So those first days on my own felt less like a separation than a reunion—I was reconnecting with myself, rediscovering parts that had lain dormant for so long that I'd forgotten all about them. Most significantly of all, that soft inner voice—the one that hadn't spoken up for so long—was now calling the shots for my life.

At first I was almost giddy from my newfound independence. I soon found, however, that the situation was a double-edged sword: When things needed to get done, I was the one who had to do them. When I heard noises in the night, I was the one who had to investigate. I was experiencing a crash course (or, actually, more like on-the-job training) in self-reliance!

More significantly than any external changes and challenges, however, I realized that the silence and solitude left me no buffer between me and myself. There was no more avoiding the enormous task of untangling myself—separating the person who I thought I was supposed to be from the person I actually was.

This, I discovered, is the work of a lifetime.

Mourning the Loss of Your Expectations

If you get separated or divorced, there's a period of mourning. You have to mourn not just for the past—the hurts, the mistakes, the anger, the pain—but also for the future.

You are mourning the loss of your expectations.

You probably expected that you'd spend the rest of your life in wedded bliss. You probably thought that your lonely days were over. You might have pictured happy scenes of you and your spouse in your golden years, surrounded by grandchildren, basking in a lifetime of happy memories and ongoing love.

No doubt about it, divorce is a death—the death of a fantasy. Death of your expected plans of family holidays, vacations and a shared future. And even if this is ultimately positive—to replace fantasy with reality—it can still be a painful process.

And this is a process that we all go through—whether we are married, divorced, widowed, or have never been married. Whenever we let go of a fantasy, a cherished hope or dream, we have to let go of part of ourselves. It can be like letting go of a favorite piece of childhood clothing—one that may have fit perfectly in the past, but no longer fits the person you've become.

The process of letting go of old dreams can be heartbreaking, but in doing so, we open a space where a more satisfying reality and a more authentic self can enter.

> *You have to mourn not just for the past—the hurts, the mistakes, the anger, the pain—but also for the future.*

Separating from Yourself

Separation and divorce are not just about married couples splitting up. Even if you are happily married or single, I ask you:

- *Do you ever feel divorced from your authentic self?*
- *Do you ever feel as if your body is just going through the motions while your soul gets pushed into a corner and out of sight?*
- *Do you ever feel so disconnected from your life that it hardly even feels like your own?*

Even people in generally happy relationships can be disconnected from themselves. Conversely, single people might feel a strong sense of inner connection.

Separation from yourself can happen in an instant—such as during a traumatic experience—or it can happen gradually over the course of many years. It can happen when you stop speaking up, when you ignore your inner voice, when you stop trying to make your outer life a reflection of your inner self.

It happens when you stop giving yourself the love you deserve.

On the positive side, however, you can *always* come back to yourself. Your soul will always be waiting to forgive and take you back with open arms. And it can happen in an instant—any instant, even this one right now!

The Gift of Forgiveness

One of the greatest obstacles to healing, growth,

and love is the reluctance to forgive.

When we are angry, hateful, or carry discord or resentment within us—toward past relationship partners or others who we feel have wronged us—we only serve to injure ourselves on many levels: mentally, physically, and spiritually. Just because a past relationship ends or falls apart doesn't mean you have to carry around negative feelings surrounding that relationship. No matter the intensity of feeling upon the termination, whether the relationship was with a parent, sibling, friend, or sexual partner, it need not scar you in your everyday life. You can choose how much of that emotional burden you wish to feel and experience, how long you want to carry that burden, and when you're ready to let it go.

Forgiveness doesn't mean that you will eliminate pain from your life. Pain is unavoidable. Injuries are a natural part of life. But so is healing. When you get cut, you bleed for a while, but fairly soon the blood starts to clot. The cut heals. And before too long, you can no longer see evidence that you'd ever been cut.

Unless you keep picking at the scab. In that case, you're likely to re-open the wound, to bleed all over again, and possibly even cause an infection. And this is exactly what you do when you keep replaying past injuries—whether they were your own fault or someone else's. Every time you replay those scenes or retell those stories, you "pick at your scabs" and re-open your own wound. You become stuck in the past. You inhibit your natural healing processes, and you rob yourself of the joy the present moment could offer you.

Letting Go

Another way of thinking of this is simply letting go of something that's hurt you. Imagine that you saw someone squeezing a hot, sharp metal blade. It's hurting them—burning and cutting their hand. The longer they hold it, the worse they burn themselves. The tighter they squeeze, the deeper their cuts.

What would you tell this person?

My guess is that you would say, "Let it go!" And if they argued that they wanted to hurt this blade, which had caused them so much pain and anguish, you'd probably be even more adamant: "Trust me—the sooner you release your grip, the sooner you can start to heal."

It might seem obvious or even ridiculous in a scenario like this, but this is exactly what so many of us do—we hold on tighter and tighter to the very thing that hurts us and, in doing so, make the injury deeper and more painful than it needs to be.

Fortunately, however, the body, mind, and spirit are very resilient. We can recover from almost anything. Even the most painful of injuries begins to heal the moment that the source of the injury is released.

So if someone tells you to "let it go," as annoying as that might sound to you, they're probably giving you great advice— for your own benefit!

Forgiving Others, Forgiving Ourselves

So often, marriages end because one partner is unable or unwilling to let go of past hurts and forgive the other. But this can cause just as much pain to individuals who are unwilling to forgive themselves—often because they feel that forgiveness means condoning an act. But nothing could be further from the truth. Forgiveness merely means that you are releasing the emotional charge that holds you in the past, that keeps you picking that scab and reopening that wound—over and over and over.

> *Forgiveness does NOT mean condoning a hurtful act. Forgiveness merely means that you are releasing the emotional charge that holds you in the past.*

As difficult as it is to forgive someone else who has wronged you, the hardest person of all to forgive might be yourself. You probably set very high expectations for yourself. You want to be perfect. You want to be good. You want to be loved—or at least liked! And when you find yourself acting without compassion or consideration—even if just for a brief moment—it's natural to judge yourself harshly. If you hurt another person—especially someone you love—that can make it even more difficult.

Yes, you may have done something hurtful. And no, you probably don't want to condone such behavior—in yourself or in anyone else. But remember, forgiveness is not the same as condoning or saying what you did was OK. It is merely admitting that you are human. You made a mistake. You will do better in the future. You are ready to release the self-inflicted pain and move forward into freedom.

Aside from the personal healing you experience when you are able to forgive yourself, it can also make you more compassionate toward others. Realizing that we all have the capacity to act horribly at times reminds us that committing a hurtful act doesn't make us a bad person. It doesn't mean that we lose the capacity to give, to love, and to live with an open heart.

And the same applies to others who may have hurt you. So even your darkest moments can serve to open your heart—to see the humanity in yourself and in others, and to forgive those

> *Are you ready to move on, to come back to the present, to come back to yourself?*

who trespass against you, just as you would like to be forgiven—by them and by yourself.

Whether you are forgiving yourself or another person, forgiveness is a gift you give yourself—the opportunity to leave the past in its place and return to the present...and to yourself. Forgiveness is the freedom you will feel when you cut the binding chains of your emotional past.

So, are you ready to move on, to come back to the present, to come back to yourself?

Remember, no matter how long you've been angry, hurting, or stewing in resentment, you can always release anything that no longer serves you. No matter how far off track you may have gotten, you can always turn things around!

"Wrong" Turns and "You" Turns

I was recently talking to my editor while driving to my son's soccer game. In the middle of the conversation, I suddenly realized I was going the wrong way.

"Oops! I took a wrong turn," I told my editor. "Can I call you back?" I hung up, turned the car around, drove back to the right road, and called back my editor.

We both thought that this wrong turn was a great metaphor because, after all: *We ALL take wrong turns sometimes!* We act irresponsibly. We make poor choices. We may settle in a relationship that is less than healthy. We get into bad relationships. We mess up good relationships. We neglect ourselves. We hurt others. We have inappropriate physical relationships out of a need for closeness. We make mistakes. In short, we act like what we are: humans!

The question is: *What do you do when this happens?*

- Do you bang on the steering wheel and curse yourself for being so careless?
- Do you blame the "stupid" road signs or faulty directions?
- Do you refuse to admit that you took a wrong turn, and obstinately continue the way you're going?
- Do you step on the gas and go speeding as fast as you can in this wrong direction?

Hopefully, you don't (although I admit I've fallen into the "blame game" on occasion).

None of these approaches helps you. They just make you feel bad, they waste your time and energy (and gas), and they certainly don't get you back on track.

The most helpful course of action is very simple and straightforward:

- First, recognize that you've taken a wrong turn—that you're heading in the wrong direction.
- If you know where you are, turn the car around until you're back on track.
- If you're lost, stop and ask for directions.

(And, of course, you have to know where you want to go!)

It seems so simple when we look at it in terms of driving, but what happens when you take "wrong turns" in your own life— actions or decisions that don't lead to your desired destination?

- Do you expend a lot of energy needlessly berating yourself or others?
- Do you deny that there's a problem—that you're not heading where you intended to go? ("Yes, of *course* I meant to drive past the exit and go over the bridge!")

- Or are you humble and wise enough to recognize the wrong turn, get help if you need it, take action to get back on track, and learn from the experience?

Most of the time, wrong turns are no big deal—especially if you catch them fairly soon. In my case, I found my way back to the soccer field and still arrived in time to see my son's game. And now I'll know the way for next time—and I'll be able to help anyone else who might need directions (including what to watch out for: e.g., "If you see a post office, you've gone too far!").

Also, remember that sometimes "wrong turns" can lead you somewhere even more wonderful than your original intended destination. Sometimes, "mistakes" can turn out to be some of the most fortuitous events of your life. So don't be too quick to label something a "wrong turn"—even if it feels that way at first.

But even if it is a wrong turn, that's OK, too. Unlike most highways and busy intersections, in life, U-turns (or "you-turns") are always permitted!

I knew I should've made that left turn in Albuquerque!

Reunion and Renewal

My separation was a time of extreme growth on my part—and also a lesson in humility. I had to acknowledge my own role in the breakdown of my marriage. I had to acknowledge that I had been responsible for my life. I even had to acknowledge that I had been horrible at times.

But, oddly enough, this opened my heart to extreme compassion. By realizing that I was capable of trespassing, I felt it easier to forgive others for their trespasses. I was able to recognize the common humanity—between myself, my husband, and everyone who had ever hurt me.

I also learned to appreciate my husband—for everything he had done for me, and for the person he was (and is). And, I'm happy to say, he also learned to appreciate me—and not just because of all the housework he now had to do (although I'd be lying if I said that this wasn't a factor!).

After two years apart—two years of intense introspection, reflection, and growth for both of us—we decided to reunite. Although our reunion has not been without its challenges, we are now both much better equipped to face those challenges with love and compassion—for one another and for ourselves.

~ EXERCISES ~

Short Term vs. Long Term

Do you tend more toward instant gratification or delayed gratification? What are the drawbacks and/or benefits of this?

_____

_____

_____

_____

*How can you achieve a healthier balance in your focus and actions? (E.g., Not sacrificing long-term goals for short-term pleasure; or, take more time to enjoy the present rather than focusing excessively on your future.) What are some specific steps you can take to live a happier, healthier life in both the short and long term?*_____

_____

_____

_____

Projections and Reality

When have you projected qualities onto someone or something— only to realize that they were very different from your impressions/projections? _____

_____

_____

_____

*What are some qualities that others project onto you (or, perhaps that you project onto yourself) that you think might not be entirely accurate?*_____

_____

_____

_____

How can you avoid getting caught up in projections—and see reality for what it is? _____

_____

_____

Past the Finish Line

This is a chance to consider some of the major achievements or milestones in your life—whether it was a literal wedding, a graduation, promotion, or some other goal that you reached...and surpassed. This is a chance to explore that often overlooked area of what lies beyond those achievements!

*What are some of the biggest achievements or milestones you've reached in your life? Does one in particular stand out?*_____

_____

_____

_____

How did you feel AFTER you passed it? _____

_____

_____

_____

*Did you celebrate? If so, how? If not, why not?*_____

_____

_____

_____

*How did your life change afterwards? (E.g., Did you shift direction,
change your perspective, or begin focusing on a new goal?)* _____

_____

_____

_____

*What is a milestone that you've passed recently?*_____

_____

_____

*How did it feel to pass this milestone? Did you allow yourself to
experience the "inbetween-ness" after finishing—or are you
experiencing this right now? Or did you immediately begin a new
working on project or goal?* _____

_____

_____

_____

Taking Responsibility

*When have you blamed someone else for the way you felt?*_____

_____

_____

_____

_____

How might the situation (or your experience of it) have been different if you'd taken responsibility? _____

_____

_____

_____

When have you felt shame? Did it pass quickly, or did you wallow in it? _____

_____

_____

_____

How might your experience have been different if you'd let go of the shame sooner? _____

_____

_____

_____

Saying Goodbye to Fantasy

What cherished fantasy (perhaps a literal marriage or some other vision of happiness) have you had to let go of? _____

_____

_____

_____

Is there anything that you're holding onto that perhaps once fit you but no longer matches your true, present self? _____

_____

_____

_____

What new, positive realities might fill the space once occupied by old fantasies? _____

_____

_____

_____

_____

Returning to Yourself

*When have you felt most connected to yourself? The most alive? The most like YOU?*_____

_____

_____

_____

_____

When have you felt the most disconnected *from yourself?*_____

_____

_____

_____

_____

What are you most passionate about? What brings you to life? How can you bring that passion into your life more and more?

_____

_____

_____

_____

_____

Forgiving, Healing, and Moving On

Who do you have the hardest time forgiving? What if you did forgive them? (Remember, forgiving doesn't mean condoning, it just means releasing the charge so you can get on with your life!)

_____

_____

_____

_____

_____

What do you want or need to forgive yourself for? (E.g., did you steal or lie? Were you selfish? Did you fail to give someone what they needed?) Can you forgive yourself? Can you do it right now?

_____

_____

_____

_____

_____

How might your life be different if you were able to forgive and release all past hurts? Can you forgive those that hurt you the most? (Again, remember, this doesn't mean that you forget or condone them—it just means that they no longer have a charge, they no longer have a hold on you.) _____

_____

_____

_____

_____

_____

"Wrong" Turns

When was the last time you made a "wrong turn" in your life? How did you get back on track? _____

_____

_____

_____

_____

_____

Have you ever made a "wrong turn" that led somewhere even better than where you'd planned to go? _____

_____

_____

_____

_____

_____

Returning to You

So, after you've made the entire TMITW journey—from meeting and courtship to engagement and marriage, and perhaps even overcome a bump of separation—what's left?

To keep saying yes to yourself. To keep growing. And to keep coming back—*again and again and again...*

Afterglow

Renewing Your Vows

~ Saying "Yes" to Yourself...Again ~

Now that you have gone through the *To Me I Thee Wed* process, I would like to leave you with one final suggestion:

Let your love be alive!

By this, I mean *let it grow, change, live, and breathe.* Be open to change. Don't feel trapped by old, outdated habits, beliefs, or vows. You are not the same person you were 10 or 20 years ago, and your life should reflect that! Allow your love and your life to reflect the person you are today!

> ## You are not the same person you were 10 or 20 years ago, and your life should reflect that!

Relationship Reflection

Just as you check in with your financial situation (checking your bank account balance, or just mentally tallying your bills and expenses), check in with yourself on a regular basis.

In a literal marriage, this might include asking if you're relating well to one another, or seeing if there's anything that you'd like to express to one another. Regarding yourself as an individual, this might mean checking in and connecting with yourself—asking yourself if you're on track, living the life you want to live, expressing your true authentic self, and taking time to connect with that person underneath all of the masks.

Revisiting and Renewing Your Vows

This process can also mean revisiting and renewing your vows—either literal wedding vows or the ones you've made to yourself. If you do this regularly, you might find that many of your old priorities are not as important to you as they once were, while many new values may have replaced the ones you've let go.

Your vows should never be "written in stone." Let them breathe, live, and grow—just like yourself!

Being your own best friend means not just allowing yourself to change and grow, but encouraging it—celebrating it! Being your own ideal partner (your own "better half"...or "best whole"!) means loving yourself for exactly the person you are right now, in each and every moment—unconditionally, forever.

~~~~~~

Exercise: Revisiting and Rewriting Your Vows

After a year (or any amount of time that feels right to you), revisit the vows you wrote to yourself. What parts still apply? What parts no longer reflect the person you are today? (You also might want to update your vision board regularly with elements of your personal vows and self-love visions.) _____

_____

_____

_____

Rewrite your vows—updating them to reflect who you are now.

(Repeat this process regularly—as long as you live.)

Twenty Years and a Second Chance

Having been reunited for several years, my husband and I took a 20th anniversary trip to St. Lucia.

It was exotic and beautiful—a tropical paradise. (Weather-wise, it was the polar opposite of our honeymoon ski trip!) We spent a week in a private cabin on a sugar plantation. To be perfectly honest, it wasn't the most relaxing week of my life—filled as it was with mosquito nets, cow pastures, and only the bare necessities—but it was certainly one of the most interesting and memorable weeks of my life!

One day near the end of the trip, my husband told me that we were going on a tour of the plantation. After taking a quick shower, I made myself as pretty as I could manage in front of the outdoor mirror. With my hair still wet, I set off with my husband, hand in hand.

The owner showed us around the plantation, telling us bits and pieces about the plantation's history and operation—but I soon realized that this tour was not the evening's main event.

As we walked around the corner, I saw a six-foot, colorful flower arrangement and two beautiful local women—one of them about twice the size of the other—sitting on a nearby bench. The larger woman stood up and shook my hand with an assured grip and an authentic smile. I was informed that she was a Justice of the Peace and that she was there to marry us for the second time.

I turned to my husband, unchecked tears flowing down my face. Rick had only seen me cry about five times in twenty years, so he definitely realized how special this moment was—for both of us!

And it was absolutely perfect: just us and our moment, unencumbered by expectations. Even with the tears flooding my face, I managed to say my impromptu vows, to summarize my feelings for this man for the last 20+ years, to express everything that I had felt and received from him. The honesty was overwhelming, the truth was assured, and the moment was perfect.

Although our wedding was very beautiful (or so I've been told!), when we said our vows for the second time, it felt so much more authentic. This time I didn't have to plan. I wasn't nervous. And I hadn't been having nightmares about the moment! This time around, there was no checking out or dissociation.

This time I was fully present.

I was emotionally connected.

I was me.

Resources and Recommendations

These are just a handful of the books that have helped to inform my work and my life. I heartily recommend them to anyone interested in further reading in these areas.

Mitch Albom, *The Five People You Meet in Heaven* and *Tuesdays with Morrie*

Steve Andreas and Charles Faulkner, *NLP: The New Technology of Achievement*

John Bradshaw, *Healing the Shame that Binds You*

Leo Buscaglia, *Living, Loving, Learning*; *Loving Each Other*; and *Born for Love*

Julia Cameron, *The Artist's Way: A Path to Higher Creativity*

Emerson Eggerichs, *Love and Respect: The Love She Most Desires, the Respect He Desperately Needs*

David G. Evans, *Healed Without Scars*

Michael J. Gelb, *How to Think like Leonardo da Vinci: Seven Steps to Genius Every Day*

William F. Harley, Jr., *His Needs, Her Needs*

Gay Hendricks, *The Big Leap: Conquer Your Hidden Fear and Take Life to the Next Level*

Steven C Hayes, Ph.D., with Spencer Smith, *Get Out of Your Mind and Into Your Life: The New Acceptance and Commitment Therapy*

Harville Hendrix and Helen LaKelly, *Giving the Love That Heals* and *Getting the Love You Want*

Muriel James and Dorothy Jongeward, *Born to Win: Transactional Analysis with Gestalt Experiments*

Wendy Lipton Dibner, *Shatter Your Speed Limits*

Martin Seligman, *Learned Optimism: How to Change Your Mind and Your Life*

Rick Warren, *The Purpose-Driven Life*

Index

About the Author

Julia Bowlin, M.D.

JULIA BOWLIN, M.D., was born and raised in Darke County, Ohio, and has lived in the area most of her life. Her undergraduate degree in Socio-Anthropology was received at Earlham College in Indiana in 1988. She attended Wright State University School of Medicine in Dayton, Ohio, and received her M.D. in June, 1993.

Dr. Bowlin did her family medicine residency at St. Elizabeth Hospital in Dayton, Ohio, and went on to become the owner and medical director of Versailles Medical Center in Versailles, Ohio.

She is married to Rick Bowlin, M.D., a local practicing internal medicine physician. Together they have two children and presently reside in Greenville, Ohio.

Dr. Julia Bowlin's struggle with depression, eating disorders, and self-harming behaviors as an adolescent and young adult has afforded her personal insight into what it is like to have a poor view of one's inner self and feel divorced from herself. Because of her past emotional struggles, her Bachelor of Arts degree in Socio-Anthropology, and her Doctorate of Medicine degree, she has an intimate as well as a professional understanding of how personal, social, and cultural influences can impact one's inner self. She has a fresh perspective and approach to guiding you towards excavating your best inner self, using common sense ideas, traditional values, and modern understanding.

~ For more information, please visit www.juliabowlinmd.com. ~

www.ingramcontent.com/pod-product-compliance
Lightning Source LLC
Chambersburg PA
CBHW031126090426
42738CB00008B/990